World Tourism Organization

Market Intelligence and Promotion Section

Sustainable Tourism Development Section

Madrid, October 2002

The Spanish Ecotourism Marke'

Special Report, Number 14

Capitán Haya 42
28020 Madrid
Tel: (34) 91 567 81 00
Fax: (34) 91 571 37 33
E-mail: omt@world-tourism.org
Internet: www.world-tourism.org

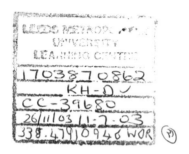
Copyright 2002 World Tourism Organization

The Spanish Ecotourism Market

ISBN: 92-844-0547-5

Published by the World Tourism Organization
Madrid, Spain

Printed by the World Tourism Organization. Madrid, Spain

Foreword

Background

In view of the sustained growth of tourism activity world-wide, it would be reasonable to assume that the ecotourism sector will develop along parallel lines. However, no extensive international market research has hitherto been conducted with a view to corroborating this hypothesis.

On the occasion of the designation by the United Nations of 2002 as the International Year of Ecotourism (IYE), the World Tourism Organization (WTO) has decided to undertake research with a view to increasing knowledge of the following seven countries in their capacity as ecotourism generating markets: Germany, USA, United Kingdom, Canada, Spain, France and Italy[1].

Market studies of this type must be based on a coordinated approach among the experts concerned, similar research methods and, more importantly, a common concept of the term «ecotourism» if they are to deliver well-founded conclusions and global recommendations. However, concepts of ecotourism clearly vary, not only from one country to another, but also within the same territory. Likewise, the specific attributes of each of the markets studied, the availability of tour operators to respond to surveys depending on whether they were run in peak or low seasons and the inclusion of ecotourism products in more general products do not permit a strict comparability of the different studies presented in this series of monographs.

Readers are therefore asked to consider the results of these studies as general trends relative to the ecotourism market, rather than absolute reference data. This is the first time that such researches have been initiated. These are pioneer studies, whose methodology and results can serve as basis for future researches in this topic.

---

1   Another WTO publication, prepared with the technical contributions of its Member States, is also devoted to the IYE. This publication, titled as " Sustainable Development of Ecotourism: A Compilation of Good Practices" (ISBN: 92-844-0478-9), contains 55 case studies from 39 countries.

Aims, definitions and methodology

After briefly summarizing the general characteristics of tourism markets, these surveys set out to analyse and evaluate, in each of the aforementioned countries, the nature tourism and ecotourism generating market, its volume, characteristics, major trends and development prospects, consumer profiles, the role of the different marketing actors, product typologies and the main communication and marketing tools used in these markets.

It was with a view to meeting these aims that WTO hired seven experts – one per country – all of whom adopted similar research methods:

- gathering the results of existing research studies with the aim of making an initial appraisal of the volume of this market;

- running consumer surveys based on a single questionnaire for all countries with a view to studying demand trends;

- running surveys among tour operators whose policies and products are commensurate, to some extent at least, with ecotourism concepts;

- studying the catalogues and brochures put out by these tour operators;

- organizing tour operator discussion forums (or focus groups) on the occasion of tourism trade fairs with a view to comparing marketing methods and results, but also with the aim of discussing the very notion of ecotourism.

It should also be noted that the same definition of ecotourism was used by all the different experts. WTO has defined this activity at two levels:

1. Nature tourism: a form of tourism in which the main motivation is the observation and appreciation of nature.

2. Ecotourism: a form of tourism with the following characteristics:

   i. All nature-based forms of tourism in which the main motivation of the tourists is the observation and appreciation of nature as well as the traditional cultures prevailing in natural areas.

   ii. It contains educational and interpretation features.

   iii. It is generally, but not exclusively, organised for small groups by specialized and small locally-owned businesses. Foreign operators of varying sizes also organize, operate and/or market ecotourism tours, generally for small groups.

iv. It minimizes negative impacts on the natural and socio-cultural environment.

v. It supports the protection of natural areas by:

- generating economic benefits for host communities, organizations and authorities that are responsible for conserving natural areas;

- creating jobs and income opportunities for local communities; and

- increasing awareness both among locals and tourists of the need to conserve natural and cultural assets.

The most outstanding results of the seven studies can be summed up as follows

1. The use of the term «ecotourism» in the marketing and promotional tools and used by tour operators is still relatively limited. It would appear that this term has not yet been integrated in the marketing strategies of the nature tourism sector.

2. Likewise, the tourism sector that most closely matches the concept of ecotourism represents a relatively small share of the market, an observation that is borne out by the small dimension of the tour operators that comprise this segment and the small number of tourists they cater for.

3. Conversely, these same tour operators apparently believe that the growth of ecotourism may outpace that of other tourism activities overall. Moreover, this growth appears to be consolidating irrespective of the destination considered. A priori, no world region appears to have a head-start although each region does have several landmark destinations.

4. The surveys conducted among the various audiences show that enthusiasm for nature tourism invariably goes hand-in-hand with a desire for meeting local communities and discovering different facets of their culture (gastronomy, handicrafts, customs, etc.).

5. According to tour operators, ecotourism enthusiasts are mostly people from relatively high social brackets and with relatively high levels of education; they are over 35 and women slightly outnumber men.

6. These studies also show that environmental awareness, while still in its infancy, is clearly growing.

As mentioned above, these initial findings must be confirmed on the basis of future studies. These preparatory surveys should nonetheless provide a springboard for a more in-depth examination of ecotourism markets, which will be one of the key elements of the World Ecotourism Summit to be held in Quebec, Canada, from 19 to 22 May 2002.

Acknowledgements

The World Tourism Organisation wishes to express its gratitude to Mr. Juan Carlos Torres Riesco, of Planta SA, for the preparation of this report, with the assistance of Ms. Elena Contreras and Mr. Marcello Notarianni.

The World Tourism Organisation and the authors express their gratitude to all those tour operators who generously donated their time to taking part in this research, answering the questionnaire and/or participating in the interviews carried out. They also extend their gratitude to the tourists who took part in the preparation of the study.

The research for preparing this study was carried out by a group of experts to whom the WTO entrusted the task, under the supervision of Mr. Eugenio Yunis, Head of the Sustainable Development of Tourism Section and Mr. Augusto Huéscar, Head of the Market Intelligence and Promotion Section. The final check was carried out by Mr. Philippe Lemaistre, WTO Programme Officer.

Table of contents

Executive Summary

The Spanish ecotourism market is small and seasonal, although it is growing rapidly and shows great potential.

In Spain the term "ecotourism" is used little in the tourism market, as regards both supply and demand. Only 47% of the operators consulted declared themselves in complete agreement with the WTO's definition and only 52.36% use the term ecotourism when promoting their catalogues.

Rural, landscape and nature tourism, the segments with the most significant demand for ecotourism, account for almost 6% of income and stays/overnight stays in the Spanish tourism market as a whole (sun and beach account for 66%). As well as this, between 5 and 6% of Spanish tourist traffic abroad is estimated to have "pure" or primarily ecotourism motives. In absolute terms this market is made up of between 60,000 and 100,000 people.

The strong increase noted in visits to National Parks by Spanish residents (+ 176% in the decade 1990 – 2000 and + 26% 1997 – 2000) is an indicator of the potential of the ecotourism-motivated market.

Virtually all the operators consulted declared that their ecotourism business has grown in recent years and forecast that it will continue to do so in the coming ones.

Approximately 55% of the products offered by the TOs that have collaborated with this study are considered by them as "ecotourism packages combined with conventional content" or "mixed" packages", although a high percentage, 30%, is composed of "pure" ecotourism products, where the main motive for the trip is ecotourism.

The clients demand packages that offer a change of scenery, the chance to practise activities in contact with nature and introduce themselves into the local culture, although in general, they opt for combining these activities of a purely ecotourist nature with others, i.e., they also prefer "mixed" packages.

On these trips, or ecotourism packages, which are organized by the TOs, what is valued above all, is respect for the natural environment and that the groups of tourists are small.

Among the most popular activities in the ecotourism packages offered on the Spanish market, are the observation of fauna, nature trekking, visits to protected areas and coexistence with traditional and indigenous communities. On a second level we would find: exploration trails, sport trekking, trips of naturalist interest, natural / cultural heritage, ethnology, etc.

The duration of the ecotourism trips organized by the TOs is generally between two and three weeks for destinations outside Europe, two weeks for destinations inside Europe and one week for destinations in Spain.

The ecotourism market suffers the same problems of high seasonal variation as the Spanish conventional tourism market; as can be seen in the analysis of the interviews with operators, the majority of ecotourism packages are sold in summer (77%).

As regards the destinations offered, the bulk of ecotourism sales and trips are made outside Europe (74% of sales and 71% of trips). Latin America and Africa, in particular Namibia, Tanzania and Botswana in Africa, and Guatemala, Peru and Argentina in Latin America stand out as the most common destinations. As for Europe, Spain, Scandinavia and almost all of Spain's neighbouring countries feature prominently.

From the point of view of demand, the majority of tourists also prefer distant countries, outside Europe for ecotourism-type trips. (42% of the total). Nevertheless, Europe, and in particular Spain, are also chosen by a large percentage of clients.

Among the destinations abroad, one can perceive a clear preference for Latin American and African countries, with Brazil and Argentina featuring prominently, followed by Mexico and Cuba. Other destinations very much in demand are in Asia, such as India and Nepal. Countries such as Australia or Egypt are also chosen by a significant percentage of ecotourists.

In Europe, the following destinations stand out; Italy, the Scandinavian and Nordic countries, France, Great Britain, The Alps and Greece.

As for domestic tourism, within Spain 38% of tourists surveyed prefer destinations in the North of Spain, "Green Spain" (Asturias, Galicia, Basque Country, Cantabria, etc.), or to visit National Parks (principally Doñana, Ordesa and Picos de Europa National Parks), although the islands (especially the Canaries) and Andalusia are also highly valued.

As for the profile of the Spanish ecotourism consumer, he/she is an urban traveller, young (59% between 20 and 39 years old), the majority are women (55%) and earn between 1,500 and 2,400 €/month /57%).

Among the main motives of the Spanish ecotourist, the most important are visits to protected areas and National Parks and, to a lesser extent, coexistence with the indigenous population and the contemplation of outstanding fauna and landscape.

It seems that a large number of Spanish ecotourists associate ecotourism simply with visits to protected areas. Thus, a certain lack of motivational definition exists, which is still very generic compared with that of other countries.

The financial or voluntary contribution of the Spanish tourist to the destination communities is virtually non-existent.

Respect for local culture and traditions is one of the most important aspects for the great majority of ecotourists (85%). The conservation of nature and landscape is equally important, a preserved environment makes their holidays more satisfactory and they are horrified by landscapes which have been destroyed by urban and infrastructure excesses.

Fewer than half of the tourists surveyed thought that the operator's commitment to the environment was important when choosing an operator-programme-agent.

This is an indication of the stubbornly low environmental awareness and commitment to local communities which characterize the Spanish consumer in contrast to other European markets which demonstrate far more solidarity, commitment and maturity in this respect.

I. Introduction

1.1. Objectives of the study

The United Nations has declared 2002 International Ecotourism Year. In order to prepare for it, the World Tourism Organisation (WTO) has commissioned market studies on ecotourism in the following countries: Canada, France, Germany, Italy, Spain, United Kingdom and United States. The research has been prepared as a comparative study. In each country, a common definition of ecotourism and similar methods were used.

This report explores the ecotourism market in Spain. Its objectives are to "deepen the qualitative and quantitative knowledge of the Spanish generating ecotourism market, its structure, types of products, sub-segments, profiles, marketing channels, products and star destinations".

1.2. Territorial Scope

As an analysis of the Spanish generating market, the study covers the whole of the Spanish territory, the Spanish population and the tour operators and specialized travel agencies that are based, or have their headquarters, in Spain.

The destinations of the Spanish ecotourists studied cover all the countries in the world. Spain is studied primarily as an outbound tourism country for ecotourists, but also as an inbound one. Spain is the world's number three tourist destination, with almost 50 million visitors per year, although its outbound market is very small, when compared with the other countries studied (less than 4 million trips abroad in the year 2000).

1.3. Definition of ecotourism in the context of this study

The WTO wanted the tour operators of each country to assess the following definition of Ecotourism, thus, one of the objectives of the study consisted of describing and analyzing the corresponding response received from the sector in each of the countries studied:

The World Tourism Organisation's (WTO) definition of these terms:

- **Nature Tourism:** All types of tourism based on nature, where the main motive is the observation and appreciation of nature, as well as traditional cultures.

- **Ecotourism:** Ecotourism is a type of tourism in areas rarely frequented by man, which should contribute to the protection of nature and the welfare of the local population.

  1. It should include the interpretation of nature and pedagogical aspects.

  2. Although this is not essential, it is generally organized for small groups by small local companies. Foreign operators, large and small, also organise, set in motion and/or market ecotourism routes, generally for small groups.

  3. It minimizes the negative impact on the natural and the socio-cultural environments.

  4. It provides resources for the protection of nature sites:

     - Generating economic benefits for the local communities, the organizations and the authorities that manage these sites with a view to their protection and conservation,

     - Creating jobs and generating (alternative) income for the local communities, making the local population and the tourists aware of the importance of culture and nature conservation.

1.4. Methodology and study sources

In accordance with the terms of reference, in order to achieve the results of the study, the following tasks were carried out:

1) A survey of tourists in their country of origin (Spain) who visited stands belonging to destinations with an ecotourism image during FITUR 2001, the main Spanish international tourism fair. On 3rd and 4th February, 424 surveys were carried out in FITUR in the area where diverse stands of countries with ecotourism destinations were located.

2) In-depth surveys and interviews were carried out with specialized Spanish outbound travel operators and agencies and managers of tourist offices in Madrid which had an ecotourism image and offers.

3) An analysis of specialized operators' and agencies' brochures / catalogues.

Surveys of tourists in their country of origin

The 424 surveys carried out on the basis of interviews with people of both sexes aged over 18, selected at random, while they were visiting the medium and long distance stands offering nature and ecotourism content at FITUR 2001. Precisely because the tourists were surveyed in the area of the stands of countries offering ecotourism, the responses exhibit a greater motivation for the ecotourism theme than the average obtained from other secondary sources analyzed. This "bias" present in the sample is difficult to assess and can cause some problems for the analysis, but given the reduced general motivation in the Spanish market for what is offered in the line of ecotourism and nature, we progressed in this manner, conscious of the fact that it was necessary in order to obtain higher quality responses related to the theme of the study as opposed to the relatively insignificant ones which would have been obtained working with a completely generic sample in a global market, characterized by low knowledge and motivation regarding ecotourism and in which only 8.6% travel abroad and of these, only 79% for longer than 3 days.

Interviews with operators

The Spanish operators interviewed were selected for their orientation to and specialization in ecotourism, nature tourism, adventure tourism or any of the other segments directly or indirectly included within the concept and definition of ecotourism, or due to their being a large generalist non-specialized operator, but one which includes some trips or modules which could be considered more ecotourist in their programmes, or on occasions even a specialized or theme brochure. The first group of specialized operators and agencies offer diverse profiles of ecotourism products which can be described as "pure", and the second group arrange "mixed" products which combine ecotourism modules with more conventional and general ones.

In order to carry out the interviews with the operators and agencies, firstly the questionnaire included in Annex 2 was prepared in Spanish, by consensus and agreed with the rest of the experts in charge of the other market studies in the remaining countries.

Next, using diverse sources, a database was prepared by selecting the approximately 20 operators and agencies in Spain which are really specialized in outbound ecotourism traffic, plus approximately 10 general operators (which we can call "mixed") which offer some programmes, or at least, some products oriented towards ecotourism in the sense of the WTO definition. The companies initially selected were contacted first by telephone to confirm their selection. We also verified their details and the name of their head of ecotourism or nature tourism products, or related programme in the case of the less specialized operators, to whom the objective of the study was explained and with whom an interview was requested. A letter was sent, by fax or E-mail, to the companies whose participation was confirmed following the first contact, confirming the conversation held, the objectives of the study and the request for an interview, as well as the topics to be addressed, etc.

In order to carry out the interviews, and given the relatively small number of companies, it was necessary to follow up the contacts with this reduced number of operators and agencies in order to effectively confirm and obtain the initial appointments. Finally, it was possible to survey the 18 operators in Madrid, Barcelona, Pamplona and Bilbao. Personal interviews were held with the ones in Madrid and the rest answered a postal survey completed via a prior and/or subsequent telephone conversation. This number, which may appear small in absolute terms, represents more than half of the source operators of this segment in Spain, and for this reason is considered to be a highly representative sample of the sector as far as the objectives of this study are concerned.

Interviews with directors of tourist offices of ecotourism destinations

In order to contrast the data regarding sales, traffic trends, the most active outbound operators for some destinations in the Spanish outbound tourism market and also to be able to provide the point of view and the vision from the ecotourism destinations, Planta also carried out interviews with directors of tourist offices in Madrid of countries with an ecotourism image and products, and which offered some type of specialized ecotourism and/or adventure tourism programmes for the Spanish market. The directors of the offices representing Guatemala, Mexico and Romania were interviewed using a similar questionnaire to that of the operators, but with some specific questions. (See Annex 2).

The reduced interest of the majority of Spanish operators in the term "ecotourism", together with the limited amount of time which product managers and managers in the tourist sector in general have, made more intensive collaboration with these professionals difficult and meant that they could only devote time to the interview or answering the questionnaire and the prior and subsequent informative conversations.

Comparing catalogues

Comparing catalogues is a very useful tool and is often used to analyze the positioning of one destination compared to another. Typology and range are compared as well as the number of packages offered, number and variety of products, duration of the stay, price, number of pages each catalogue devotes to the analyzed destination and its competitors, programmed periods or seasons and other indicators of interest and useful conclusions are obtained about how this destination is positioned with regard to the competition in the main programmes.

This comparison is useful and effective when comparing similar or fairly homogenous products in the same segment. For example, sun and beach packages or "all-in" packages of competing destinations, for example: Dominican Republic versus Cuba and Cancun competing for the European and Latin American sun and beach markets. It generally deals with destinations relatively close to each other and their main outbound tourism markets and, in order to be effective, should consist of comparisons of 3 to 5 competing destinations programmed and marketed on a mass scale.

When it came to comparing the planned ecotourism catalogues in this study, the enormous dispersion of destinations in the Spanish ecotourist programmes, the reduced number of Spanish operators that programme the same ecotourism destinations and that do so with a very different treatment and focus depending on different target groups, and at the same time the reduced effective traffic obtained for each programmed destination which, in many cases, only register symbolic sales during one or two weeks of the year, the enormous heterogeneity as regards duration, content, services included, quality or level of comfort of accommodation and other differentiated aspects (the programmed season, for example) create an endless range and typology of products and subproducts with very little commercial weight, and whose comparison is not significant.

Notwithstanding the above, Annex 4 includes the "analysis" of the most relevant brochures belonging to the interested operators. This analysis includes a general descriptive text, the main destinations programmed and the products included in each operator's brochure, which gives an idea of the typology of products, as well as a price reference.

II. The Spanish Tourism Sector (Global)

The basic sector data relevant to this study (market and ecotourism potentiality) is as follows and refers mainly to Spain as an outbound tourism market and not as an inbound tourism country. The sources for the majority of the data presented and discussed below come from the Institute for Tourism Studies, the Movements of Spanish Tourists, (Familitur) year 2000 and from the diagnosis and diverse preparatory works for the Integral Quality Plan for Spanish Tourism (PICTE), carried out in July-August of 1999.

2.1. Demand

Motives and activities of the resident demand

Of the 46.143.980 tourist trips made by Spaniards in 2000, 3,968,890 (8.6%) travelled abroad. The accompanying table breaks them down according to motives.

				REASON FOR THE TRIP					
	TOTAL	Work/ Business	Studies	Visiting Familiy/ Friends	Medical Treatment	Religious Reasons	Leisure/ Recreation/ Trips	Other	Do not know/ Do not remember
Total	46,143,980	2,503,660	1,493,728	9,090,351	384,345	512,933	30,845,390	1,226,693	86,877
Absolute data									
Abroad	3,968,890	344,197	109,366	438,148	3,453	103,627	2,799,127	164,224	6,747
Spain	42,175,090	2,159,462	1,384,362	8,652,203	380,892	409,306	28,046,260	1,062,468	80,130
Horizontal percentages									
Total	46,143,980	5.4	3.2	19.7	0.8	1.1	66.8	2.7	0.2
Abroad	3,968,890	8.7	2.8	11.0	0.1	2.6	70.5	4.1	0.2
Spain	42,175,090	5.1	3.3	20.5	0.9	1.0	66.5	2.5	0.2

PICTE, 2000

Among these, the holiday motive (leisure, recreation, holidays) features prominently with 66.8%. This percentage rises to 70.5% Spanish traffic abroad due to this motive. Unfortunately, no typology of motives more directly related to ecotourism is available.

According to activities carried out and their assessment, by destination and differentiating from foreign destinations, the accompanying table presents a greater breakdown which includes open-air sports with 6.9% of the whole, the only activity which can be directly related to an ecotourism motivation.

Number of trips according to activities carried out and their assessment, by destination.

		DESTINATION	
	TOTAL	Spain	Abroad
TOTAL	**46,143,980**	**42,175,270**	**3,968,713**
Shopping	22,281,380	19,741,330	2,540,050
Average rating	7.6	7.6	7.3
Vertical %	48.3	46.8	64.0
Golf	329,210	290,684	38,526
Average rating	8.0	7.8	9.4
Vertical %	0.7	0.7	1.0
Skiing	714,548	382,269	332,280
Average rating	8.3	8.0	8.7
Vertical %	1.5	0.9	8.4
Nautical Sports	1,982,042	1,854,545	127,497
Average rating	8.3	8.3	8.0
Vertical %	4.3	4.4	3.2
Hunting and Fishing	1,299,021	1,274,714	24,307
Average rating	8.0	8.0	9.4
Vertical %	2.8	3.0	0.6
Open air Sports	6,260,909	5,986,918	273,991
Average rating	8.3	8.3	8.2
Vertical %	13.6	14.2	6.9
Other Sports	2,350,301	2,223,786	126,515
Average rating	8.5	8.5	8.9
Vertical %	5.1	5.3	3.2
Major Sporting Events	1,317,069	1,181,761	135,308
Average rating	8.0	8.0	7.6
Vertical %	2.9	2.8	3.4
Major Cultural Events	5,192,846	4,397,793	795,053
Average rating	8.2	8.2	8.4
Vertical %	11.3	10.4	20.0

| | TOTAL | DESTINATION | |
		Spain	Abroad
Cultural Visits	18,010,680	15,230,200	2,780,478
Average rating	8.3	8.3	8.5
Vertical %	39.0	36.1	70.1
Theme Parks	2,683,109	2,287,198	395,911
Average rating	8.5	8.5	8.4
Vertical %	5.8	5.4	10.0
Gambling	362,539	303,990	58,549
Average rating	6.5	6.6	6.1
Vertical %	0.8	0.7	1.5
Work	1,119,985	872,885	247,099
Average rating	7.7	7.6	8.0
Vertical %	2.4	2.1	6.2
Beach Use	14,005,680	13,297,340	708,348
Average rating	8.3	8.4	8.2
Vertical %	30.4	31.5	17.8
Medical Treatment	569,323	477,528	91,794
Average rating	8.7	8.7	8.6
Vertical %	1.2	1.1	2.3
Religious Events	4,259,663	3,892,266	367,397
Average rating	8.3	8.2	8.7
Vertical %	9.2	9.2	9.3
Other Activities	4,935,635	4,665,886	269,749
Average rating	8.7	8.7	8.7
Vertical %	10.7	11.1	6.8

PICTE, 2000

Open-air sports constitute a more direct reference, although still indirect, to the ecotourism motivation, representing only 14.2% of responses in Spain, and 6.9% abroad, percentages which are tellingly low, even taking into account that it was a question with multiple responses (multi-response). A part of those who practice other open-air sports -skiing, water sports, hunting and fishing, even golf- which make up a total of around 13.2%, as well as a part of those interested in cultural visits which make up 70% can also include people with an awareness of ecotourism.

It is here, together with some of the percentages of those motivated by medical treatment (2.3%) and perhaps major cultural events (20%), where we find the base of what we can describe as the current and potential demand interested in "mixed" as opposed to "pure" ecotourism products. Based on this analysis, we could tentatively estimate that about a third of the tourists with the above motives could be included in this section, thus reaching a percentage of 30% of the total. The precision of these estimates would require a survey of the motives of Spanish tourists at source, like the ones carried out in other European countries which are described below.

Motives of the European demand that visits Spain

Among the preparatory work for the Integral Quality Plan for Spanish Tourism (PICTE) prepared in the summer of 1999, 500 residents in a series of European countries were surveyed (survey of European demand) about their perception of the destination "Spain". After asking those surveyed "would you say that you are especially interested in travelling to Spain for tourism or pleasure", the following question asked those surveyed "for what reasons would you say that you are specially interested?". Of the 11 possible responses (multi-response), the third referred to landscape/nature and the fourth to sports/sporting activities.

Unfortunately the same information is not available for Spanish residents.

Comparison of the responses to the question
"for what reasons would you say that you are specially interested?".

Question	FRANCE	GERMANY	UNITED KINGDOM
Landscape/Nature	50.38%	59.82%	21.6%
Sports/Sporting activities	7.14%	10.27%	9.6%

It can be seen that Germany presents a higher percentage of tourists who declare a special interest in landscape and nature, reaching 59.82%, followed by France with 50.38%. Germany also provides more sporting tourists, with 10.27% interested in this activity.

Landscape and nature come 3rd in terms of importance in the ranking of the 11 possible motive responses in Germany and France, and only 8th in the United Kingdom.

Spanish tourists' stays.

Of the total number of trips in Spain and abroad, only 31.9% included stays of 8 nights or more, which are the relevant ones when considering ecotourism destinations abroad. This percentage reaches 39.8% for the number of trips abroad, according to Table 1 which is included in Annex 5.

The average stay for Spaniards abroad is 9.7 nights, according to Table 2 (also in Annex 5) which includes a breakdown of average stays by motive. As is logical, the most prolonged stays occurred in the study trip section with 32.3 nights (language courses, terms or four-month periods in foreign universities or schools), followed by visits to relatives and friends with 14.5 nights. The leisure/recreation/holiday motive, within which ecotourism is included, registered an average stay of 8.5 nights.

The number of overnight stays for Spaniards travelling with a tourist package is 7.5, slightly shorter that the average stays of other markets when they travel abroad (about 14 nights for the German market, at least for destinations such as Spain and the Caribbean).

Average expenditure of Spanish tourists

The average daily expenditure per Spanish tourist abroad is 17,295 pesetas (103.95 euros) as opposed to 6,269.9 pesetas (37.68 euros) in Spain, only 36% of the previous figure.

Main destinations abroad

The breakdown of Spaniards' destinations when travelling abroad (year 2000) appears in the accompanying table.

Main destinations of Spaniards abroad

	TOTAL	Vertical %
TOTAL	3,968,890	3,968,890
Absolute data		
Total for Europe	3,038,064	76.5
Germany	207,653	5.2
Andorra	441,160	11.1
Belgium	43,583	1.1
France	885,518	22.3
Italy	414,124	10.4
Netherlands	100,789	2.5
Scandinavian countries	72,830	1.8
Portugal	452,524	11.4
United Kingdom	240,811	6.1
Rest of Europe	222,656	5.6
Total for Africa	256,128	6.5
Morocco	99,982	2.5
Rest of Africa	156,146	3.9
Total for North América	138,195	3.5
USA	132,001	3.3
Rest of North America	6,194	0.2
Total for South America	319,422	8.0
Rest of the world	204,805	5.2
Not accounted for	12,276	0.3

PICTE, 2000

Of the diagnosis prepared in 1999 prior to the Integral Quality Plan for Spanish Tourism (PICTE), based on a survey of a sample of 500 Spanish residents (survey of resident demand), the following tables and information were obtained with respect to Spaniards' preferences among diverse destinations for spending their holidays.

Main parts of the world preferred for holidays
(Time and money permitting)

		Base: 500
Regions	No.	%
Europe (Except Spain)	111	22.2
Caribbean	88	17.6
Spain	70	14.0
United States	40	8.0
North Africa/Middle East	27	5.4
Mexico	21	4.2
South America	20	4.0
Australia/New Zealand	19	3.8
Far East	15	3.0
Indian Ocean	14	2.8
Canada	12	2.4
India/Tibet	7	1.4
Indonesia	3	0.6
Africa	2	0.4
None indicated	51	10.2
TOTAL	500	100

PICTE, 2000

Taking into account South America, India/Tibet and Africa as destinations with greater ecotourism interest and more to offer, in principle, these areas represent 5.8% of Spaniards' preferences, only a part of which would be ecotourism preferences. Mexico and Canada, as well as Indonesia and even North Africa, could also attract certain Spanish ecotourists.

The accompanying table distinguishes between preferences of destination according to origin (communities), and shows some significant differences.

Main parts of the world preferred for holidays by Spanish tourists.
(Structure according to Home Regions and Destination Areas %)

Base: 500

Destination Regions	Home Autonomous Communities				
	(90) Andalusia	(77) Catalonia	(51) Comunidad Valenciana	(63) Madrid	(219) Remaining Communities
Europe (Except Spain)	32.2	18.2	25.5	25.4	17.8
Caribbean	25.5	10.4	13.7	11.1	19.6
Spain	10.0	15.6	15.7	6.3	16.9
United States	4.4	11.7	11.8	11.1	6.4
North Africa/Middle East	6.7	9.1	–	6.3	4.6
Mexico	6.7	2.6	–	7.9	3.7
South America	1.1	2.6	5.9	7.9	4.1
Australia/New Zealand	4.4	7.8	2.0	1.6	3.2
Far East	2.2	2.6	–	1.6	4.6
Indian Ocean	1.1	–	3.9	11.1	1.8
Canada	–	–	3.9	4.8	3.2
India/Tibet	–	1.3	–	1.6	2.3
Indonesia	–	2.6	–	–	0.4
Africa	–	–	–	–	0.9
None indicated	5.7	15.5	17.6	3.3	10.5
TOTAL	100	100	100	100	100

PICTE, 2000

Distribution of demand according to types of accommodation

According to the type of accommodation used by Spaniards, the accompanying table shows how only 1.9% stay in rural hotels.

Number of trips according to the type of accommodation used, by destination and duration

		DESTINATION		DURATION	
	TOTAL	Spain	Abroad	Short	Long
TOTAL	**46,143,980**	**42,175,090**	**3,968,890**	**16,727,800**	**29,416,180**

Absolut data

	TOTAL	Spain	Abroad	Short	Long
Hotel or similar	13,120,480	10,604,050	2,516,434	5,473,807	7,646,673
Tourist complex	308,987	273,160	35,826	86,633	222,353
Camping/Caravan site	2,290,710	2,139,992	150,717	1,044,038	1,246,672
Own residence/Timeshare	4,544,354	4,480,989	63,366	192,360	4,351,994
Residence rented from private person	3,754,422	3,684,446	69,977	515,251	3,239,172
Residence rented through an agency	643,811	585,842	57,969	77,869	565,942
Family/friend's residence	19,080,320	18,283,320	796,994	8,342,431	10,737,890
Specialized	429,644	390,092	39,552	112,344	317,299
Country House	892,421	872,606	19,815	468,440	423,980
Other type	1,078,831	860,591	218,240	414,622	664,210

Vertical Percentages

	TOTAL	Spain	Abroad	Short	Long
TOTAL	46,143,980	42,175,090	3,968,890	16,727,800	29,416,180
Hotel or similar	28.4	25.1	63.4	32.7	26.0
Tourist complex	0.7	0.6	0.9	0.5	0.8
Camping/Caravan site	5.0	5.1	3.8	6.2	4.2
Own residence/Timeshare	9.8	10.6	1.6	1.1	14.8
Residence rented from private person	8.1	8.7	1.8	3.1	11.0
Residence rented through an agency	1.4	1.4	1.5	0.5	1.9
Family/friend's residence	41.3	43.4	20.1	49.9	36.5
Specialized	0.9	0.9	1.0	0.7	1.1
Country House	1.9	2.1	0.5	2.8	1.4
Other type	2.3	2.0	5.5	2.5	2.3

Vertical Percentages

	TOTAL	Spain	Abroad	Short	Long
TOTAL	46,143,980	91.4	8.6	36.3	63.7
Hotel or similar	13,120,480	80.8	19.2	41.7	58.3
Tourist complex	308,987	88.4	11.6	28.0	72.0
Camping/Caravan site	2,290,710	93.4	6.6	45.6	54.4
Own residence/Timeshare	4,544,354	98.6	1.4	4.2	95.8
Residence rented from private person	3,754,422	98.1	1.9	13.7	86.3
Residence rented through an agency.	643,811	91.0	9.0	12.1	87.9
Family/friend's residence	19,080,320	95.8	4.2	43.7	56.3
Specialized	429,644	90.8	9.2	26.1	73.9
Country House	892,421	97.8	2.2	52.5	47.5
Other type	1,078,831	79.8	20.2	38.4	61.6

PICTE, 2000

Of Spaniards' trips abroad, hotel accommodation stands out with 63.4%, accommodation in relatives' or friends' residences with 20.1% and camping and caravanning with 3.8%. Accommodation in country houses or other rural tourism establishments is only used by 0.5% of the Spanish who travel abroad.

2.2. Economic structure of the Spanish tourism market

In the diagnosis prepared for the Integral Quality Plan for Spanish Tourism (PICTE), the contribution made by the tourism sector to the Spanish economy was valued at 11.02% of the G.D.P. in 1999.

In terms of stays / overnight stays, the relative economic weighting of the main segments was extrapolated to 2000, with the following approximate percentages:

1. Sun and Beach: 66%
2. Culture and heritage 7%
3. Congresses and conventions: 5%
4. Business 5%
5. Landscape and nature, protected areas 3%
6. Rural Tourism 2%
7. Snow 2%
8. Nautical 2%
9. Golf 2%
10. Treatment in thermal baths, health spas 1%
11. Various others, all less than 1%, 5%

Despite the apparent greater supply and demand of rural tourism in Spain, its economic weight is still relatively insignificant in the global context of the tourism sector, accounting for around 2% of the sector's economic weight. Adding the stays connected to the main motives of landscape, nature, visits to protected areas, etc., 3% is added, so that on the whole, we could talk about 5% of the total for the sector as an indicator of preferred motives of Spanish tourist demand with regard to ecotourism.

In order to obtain an economic reference in absolute terms and in economic units about what each of these segments, in total 66,111.11 million euros (11,000 billion pesetas), represents for the Spanish tourism economy, the following approximate breakdown obtained from the same sources cited above is included:

1. Sun and Beach: 39,065.12 million euros (6,500 billion pesetas (*)).
2. Culture and heritage: 7,212.12 million euros (1,200 billion).
3. Congresses and conventions: 3,606.1 million euros (600 billion pesetas).
4. Business: 4,808.1 million euros (800 billion pesetas).
5. Landscape and nature, protected areas % 1.803 million euros (300 billion pesetas).
6. Rural Tourism 1,803 million euros (300 billion pesetas).
7. Snow 2% 1,803 million euros (300 billion pesetas).
8. Nautical 2% 1,803 million euros (300 billion pesetas).
9. Golf 2% 2,404 million euros (400 billion pesetas).
10. Treatment in thermal baths, health spas 601 million euros (100 billion pesetas).
11. Various others: 3,005 million euros (500 billion pesetas).

As regards income share, the previous order of percentages by number of stays changes due to the unequal economic added value which each segment brings to the total of tourism income. Rural Tourism improves its position slightly, increasing its representation to almost 3% of the total. Together with landscape and nature, it approaches 6% of income.

2.3. Conclusions about the Spanish tourism market (global)

By crossing all the previous data and information, we obtain the following general conclusions about the tourism market, and in particular, about the relevant Spanish tourism demand for this study:

1. The Spanish outbound tourism market is still young and small. Very small if we compare it to that of the other European countries included in this study (Germany, United Kingdom, France, Italy).

2. Only 8.6% of all Spanish tourist trips is outbound traffic for foreign countries (3,968,890 trips, 9% of what the German market contributes with 44 million trips abroad) and only about 32% of these are for stays of 8 days or more which are the relevant ones as far as Spain's ecotourism potential as an outbound market is concerned. If we reduce the band to 16 days or more, taking into account the potential of more distant or remote destinations and ecotourism products and activities requiring a longer duration, due to a longer approach, acclimatization, specific coexistence or any other aspect of the product, only 480,279 trips, or 12% of the total Spanish tourist traffic abroad, is recorded.

(*) One billion is used in Spain to denominate one million. 1 billion pesetas = 6,010.1 million euros (1 euro = 166.386 pesetas)

3. If we add the consideration of the motives, an average of only 70.5% of this traffic abroad would be of a holiday type. At the same time, only a small part of this holiday-motivated traffic would have motives or preferences connected to ecotourism awareness related to nature, culture and local communities, etc. In the next chapter on the Spanish ecotourism market, we go into this section in greater depth when analyzing, in particular, the domestic segments of rural tourism and nature tourism, protected areas, etc. For the moment, as an indication we can disclose that considering the weight of the stays / overnight stays in Spain, adding the motives of rural, landscape / nature tourism, these make up 5% and almost 6% of the total for the sector in terms of income. Therefore with the information analyzed up to now, we could estimate indirectly that between 5 and 6% of this traffic would be the current dimension of Spanish outbound tourist traffic motivated primarily or "purely" by ecotourism. Taking into account only the trips of 8 days or more, we would have a figure of less than 100,000 travellers per year (63,501). A percentage in the region of 5-6% is also obtained in the analysis of the traffic according to the destinations of a clearly ecotourist nature, although this indication is less direct and less significant.

4. The average stay of Spaniards abroad is low. 9.7 nights overall, 8.5 nights for the holiday segment in general, and 7.5 nights for package trips through operators. As it was pointed out earlier, it is significant that the stay is shorter than in other markets.

5. It is still a highly seasonal market, in which July and August account for around 70% of the activity for the year.

6. Perhaps the only positive trait of the Spanish outbound tourism market is its relatively high average expenditure of 17,295,- pesetas (103.95 euros) / day. The Spaniard does not go abroad often, or for long periods, but when he does, he spends.

III. The Spanish Ecotourism Market

3.1. Introduction

Just as in France, Germany and the United Kingdom, in Spain there are no specific complete studies of the ecotourism market or its potential.

Due to this, and just as with the other countries, it would be necessary to base oneself on studies of rural tourism and nature tourism and on other indicators of these areas to obtain indirect estimates of the Spanish ecotourism market and its potential. But, for example, even the studies about rural tourism which are regularly published across Spain, deal with supply and other aspects -quality, regulations, training-, but never analyze demand. This is only studied in some detail in works about specific areas or regions of a limited Territorial Scope - generally regions- which cannot be used as references for all Spain.

Given this situation, the surveys of 424 source tourists in Fitur included in this study, as well as the interviews held with the specialized operators and agencies and managers of tourist offices, are the only direct sources available about this segment, and for this reason are especially important as a contribution to greater qualitative and quantitative knowledge of the Spanish ecotourism market to which the WTO contributes significantly with this study.

3.2. Spanish ecotourism demand in the available secondary sources

Below is a brief analysis of some of the secondary sources which can provide additional references and indications about the Spanish ecotourism market to add to those presented in the previous chapter.

The demand for rural tourism in Spain

From the doctoral thesis "The Rural Tourism demand in Spain. With special reference to the Province of Málaga", by Rafael Fuentes García (Málaga 1994), the following information relevant to this study is given:

- 20.6% of tourists surveyed (sample of 1,466 residents) declare that they take part in rural tourism in Spain on a regular basis.

- Only 7.8% of tourists in Spain visit the Nature Reserves.

- The environmental motive is the main reason for visiting rural areas, accounting for a fifth of the responses of tourists in Spain.

- The most important age bands are those of between 20 and 28 years of age (young) and another identical percentage of 22.7%, have between 36 and 46 years of age (mature).

- Only 5% of tourists visit the inland part of Málaga province and its rural areas, they do so through a travel agent.

- The tourists in rural areas are active. 25% go horse riding and over 20% go on walks. 86% demand to carry out more than one activity.

- Three quarters of the demand for rural tourism areas is intra-regional.

- The cultural level of the tourists in rural areas is high.

- Rural tourism is very seasonal: In effect, rural tourism in Spain, even today, is limited to weekends and long weekends in spring, early autumn and the school holidays in Easter Week. In the summer holidays, the majority of the demand opting for rural tourism during the rest of the year, chooses more distant, and generally coastal destinations, and for this reason many rural tourism regions do not present high occupation coefficients in summer either. The three winter months and the working days during the length of the year register virtually no overnight stays.

- Tourists coming from Catalonia, Navarre and Cantabria are the ones who declare that nature is their main motive.

The demand for nature tourism in Spain: visits to protected areas

Andrés Iriso, in an article on "Ecotourism and nature tourism" published in "Spanish Tourism in 1998" (AECIT, 1999) includes a table of demand for some Spanish nature reserves, totalling 4,749,114 visitors in 1997 compared with 4,677,816 visitors in 1996 (97/96 + 2%). This table only includes nature reserves in 4 of the 17 existing autonomous communities, and can account for around 1/3 of the offer which attracts a figure lower than the demand which the editorial team of this study estimates in the region of 20-25% of the national total.

**VISITORS TO SOME NATURE RESERVES
(EVOLUTION 1996-97)**

Nature Reserve	Autonomous Community	1996	1997
P. N. de sa Dragonera	Balearic Islands	40.006	64.743
P. N. Cañón del Río Lobos	Castilla y León	173.730	271.906
P. N. de Sanabria (1)	Castilla y León	348.599	320.257
P. N. Lagunas de Villafáfila (2)	Castilla y León	47.002	57.280
P. N. Hoces del Duratón (2)	Castilla y León	54.458	55.940
P. N. Cadí-Moxeiró	Catalonia	330.000	300.000
P. N. Aiguamolls de l'Empordà	Catalonia	180.000	155.000
P. N. Delta de l'Ebre	Catalonia	830.000	850.000
P. N. Montserrat	Catalonia	2.500.000	2.500.000
P. N. Zona Volcánica La Garrotxa (2)	Catalonia	97.390	88.190
P. N. Señorío de Bértiz	Navarre	76.631	85.798

Source: Officials of the Autonomous Adinistrations and the Nature Reserves themselves

(1) data referring to the months of July, August and September

(2) visitor data in the information centres

The National Parks of Spain present the following evolution of visitors (values in thousands of people):

1990	1991	1992	1993	1994	1995	1996	1997	1998	1999	2000
3,716	5,402	5,626	6,237	6,765	6,807	8,123	8,123	9,042	N.D.	10,253

Source: Autonomous Body of National Parks.

This means an increase of 176% during this decade, with growth rates maintained in recent years: an increase of 26% from 1997 to 2000.

Not all visitors to National Parks are residents in Spain, we cannot therefore obtain data about the percentage of Spaniards visiting the Parks, which would be an interesting indicator in this respect. The National Parks in the Canary and Balearic Islands in particular, as well as the ones near borders (Ordesa N.P.), are visited by a percentage of non residents which the National Parks Service is ignorant of as it does not break down this concept.

3.3. Quantitative analysis of the Spanish ecotourism market

Size of the ecotourism market

In accordance with the conclusions of Chapter II, based on the analysis of the available secondary sources discussed there, Spanish outbound tourist traffic with a "pure" ecotourism motive (as has been used throughout this study), can be estimated as making up 5 to 6% of all outbound traffic. Taking into account trips of 8 days or more as the most significant for international ecotourism destinations (diagram 1), but without establishing a completely rigid cut-off point in this respect, the market can be estimated as having between 60,000 and 100,000 tourists.

Diagram 1. Duration of ecotourism trips

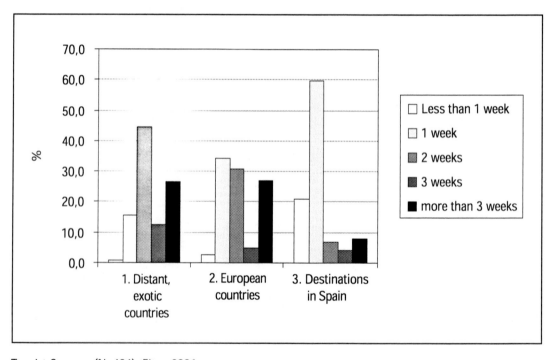

Tourist Surveys (N=424), Fitur 2001

Based on the conversations held with managers of Spanish agencies and operators specialized in ecotourism products on the occasion of the in-depth surveys, it is also confirmed that the Spanish market for what can be called "pure ecotourists" is very small. All together, the specialized Spanish operators move between 20,000 and 25,000 passengers per year according to their own sources. Taking into account that according to estimates from this sector, only around 25% of ecotourists and adventure tourists in Spain organize their holidays through an agency (Diagram 2), we can estimate that the Spanish ecotourism market (in its purest or strictest sense) is situated at between 80,000 and 100,000 people, a result which is in line with the same level obtained through the secondary sources presented in the previous paragraph.

Diagram 2. Method of reserving ecotourism trips

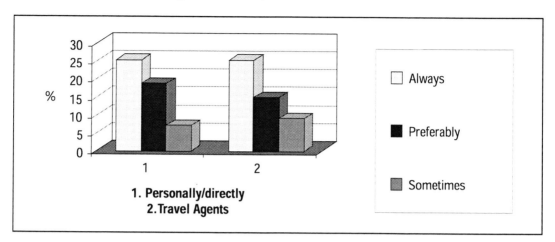

1. Personally/directly
2. Travel Agents

Tourist Surveys (N=424), FITUR 2001

Diagram 3 shows the travellers' dedication to ecotourism issues. 17.5% of those interviewed in Fitur, when answering question 9 of the questionnaire (Annex 1), declared that they devote "the maximum time possible to the observation of wild fauna and/or to the enjoyment of the natural landscape on foot or by bicycle, etc. and the rest of the activities are secondary". This must be assessed as the result of a sample of a collective contacted by the surveyors in the area around the ecotourism destination stands, and is therefore more aware of or interested in ecotourism themes or in products with an ecotourism profile than the majority.

Diagram 3. Type of dedication on the trips

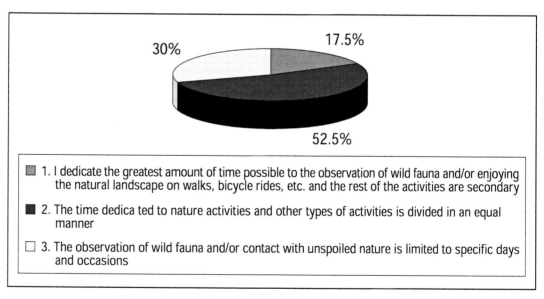

1. I dedicate the greatest amount of time possible to the observation of wild fauna and/or enjoying the natural landscape on walks, bicycle rides, etc. and the rest of the activities are secondary

2. The time dedica ted to nature activities and other types of activities is divided in an equal manner

3. The observation of wild fauna and/or contact with unspoiled nature is limited to specific days and occasions

Tourist Surveys (N=424), FITUR 2001

This greater awareness shown by the sample surveyed in Fitur, with regard to the ecotourism market previously estimated, can also be confirmed by the fact that 85% of those surveyed had already been on some type of ecotourism trip (diagram 4), and also by the high percentage of these people, 38.65%, who, as diagram 5 demonstrates, took ecotourism motives into account when they last went on holiday.

Diagram 4. Have you been on an ecotourism trip?

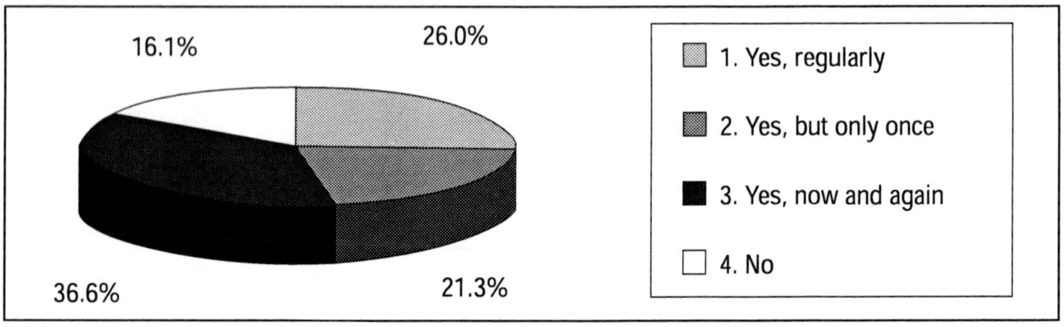

16.1%
26.0%
36.6%
21.3%
1. Yes, regularly
2. Yes, but only once
3. Yes, now and again
4. No

Tourist Surveys (N=424), FITUR 2001

Diagram 5. Main reasons for choosing the destination of the surveyed person's holiday

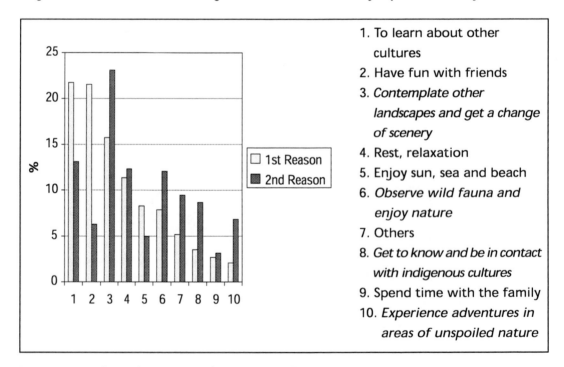

%
25
20
15
10
5
0
1 2 3 4 5 6 7 8 9 10
1st Reason
2nd Reason
1. To learn about other cultures
2. Have fun with friends
3. Contemplate other landscapes and get a change of scenery
4. Rest, relaxation
5. Enjoy sun, sea and beach
6. Observe wild fauna and enjoy nature
7. Others
8. Get to know and be in contact with indigenous cultures
9. Spend time with the family
10. Experience adventures in areas of unspoiled nature

Tourist Surveys (N=424), FITUR 2001(multi-response)

Table 1. Breakdown-motives

	Responses	% (s/864)
Ecotourism motives	334	38.7
Other motives	530	61.3
Total motives	**864**	**100**

Ecotourism motives	Responses	%(s/334)
Contemplate other landscapes and get a change of scenery	164	49
Observe wild fauna and enjoy nature	84	25
Get to know and contact indigenous cultures	50	15
Experience adventures in areas of unspoiled nature	36	11
Total ecotourism responses	**334**	**100**

The figures about "pure" ecotourism demand dealt with above are much lower than those of other European markets where specialized operators move, some of them, almost as many passengers as total number of Spaniards that go through the 25 specialized Spanish agencies. It is therefore still a very small market and one which, as we will see, suffers from the same problems of high seasonal variation as the conventional Spanish tourist market.

If, instead of considering only the trips of 8 days or more, of the 3.9 million trips which the Spanish made abroad in the year 2000 and discounting the 21% of short 1 to 3 day visits and shopping trips across the borders to Portugal, France and Andorra, we find that the Spanish international ecotourism outbound market can be estimated at 3% of the total Spanish international outbound tourist market.

The market is significantly enlarged if we include those travellers who are interested in nature, the observation of fauna and learning about other cultures, but as a secondary motive, not the main one. These are the consumers of "mixed" packages as we have called them in this study, with some nature or ecotourism component of greater or lesser significance, but within a dominantly conventional programme- This market could reach 25% of the total Spanish outbound tourism market based on the different indicators obtained and weighted.

Growth and potential of the Spanish ecotourism market

Both markets, the purer ecotourism one and the more general and conventional one which demand or appreciate ecotourism or pseudo-ecotourism modules, are growing rapidly according to those interviewed, faster than the average market growth. It can be observed that the ecotourism opportunities offered by Spanish tour operators and travel agencies, have also increased rapidly in recent years, and it is anticipated that they will continue to increase.

Diagram 6. Evolution of the amount of business of the tour operators in the last 3 years with respect to what they generally offer and what they offer in the line of ecotourism.

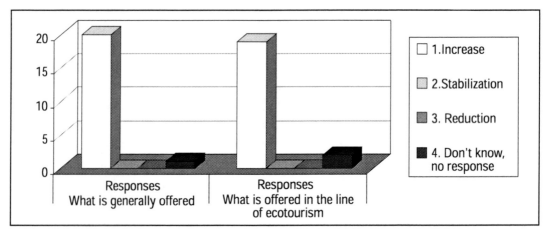

TO Survey (N=21), Planta 2001

Diagram 7. Forecast of the evolution of the ecotourism segment in what tour operators offer in the coming years

TO Survey(N=21), Planta 2001

As regards the potential of the Spanish ecotourism market, the evolution and numbers corresponding to domestic Spanish rural tourism are indicative in this respect. In principle, it seems reasonable to assume that a good number of those who practice rural tourism in Spain at present, many of them still quite young, may, in the future when they are older and have more resources and travelling culture, make up the Spanish source ecotourism market in 15 or 20 years time. The approximately 43,000 beds currently registered in Spain in rural tourism establishments, with real occupation coefficients of around 35% throughout the year, represent about 5.5 million trips or stays, the majority of which are of short duration and with 2 or 3 annual repetitions per tourist. The higher band of this market which demands the best rural tourism houses and hotels, with costs per night of over 10,000 ptas./room (around 60 euros) and which can be estimated at representing 10-12% of the whole, can provide an indirect reference about the potential of the Spanish ecotourism market with the economic capacity to permit it to leave Spain for ecotourism destinations in the future, although it is necessary to discount the effect of annual repeat trips per visitor.

The significant increase which has taken place in recent years in visits to National Parks (+ 26% 97/2000) is yet another indicator of the potential of the Spanish outbound tourism market motivated by nature, which constitutes an ecotourist reserve of great potential for destinations with nature and ecotourism related products.

3.4 Typology of ecotourism products

Due to the lack of consensus and precision regarding the term 'ecotourism' in the Spanish market, problems also exist when it comes to determining which products are, and which are not, ecotourism products. We will attempt to define the main characteristics of these products below.

Products programmed by tour operators

Approximately 55% of products offered by the tour operators who collaborated with this study are considered by the operators as "ecotourism packages combined with conventional content or "mixed" packages, although a high percentage, 30%, refers to "pure" ecotourism products, where the main motive for the trip is ecotourism. (Diagram 8). The clients demand packages that offer a change of scenery, the chance to practise activities in contact with nature and introduce themselves into the local culture, although in general, they opt for combining these activities of a purely ecotourist nature with others, i.e., they also prefer "mixed" packages.

Diagram 8. Products / packages offered by the tour operators

15%   30%   55%

1. Pure ecotourism products, where the main motive for the trip is ecotourism
2. Ecotourism products shared with conventional content at 50%
3. Conventional packages with a few days or an excursion with an ecotourism content

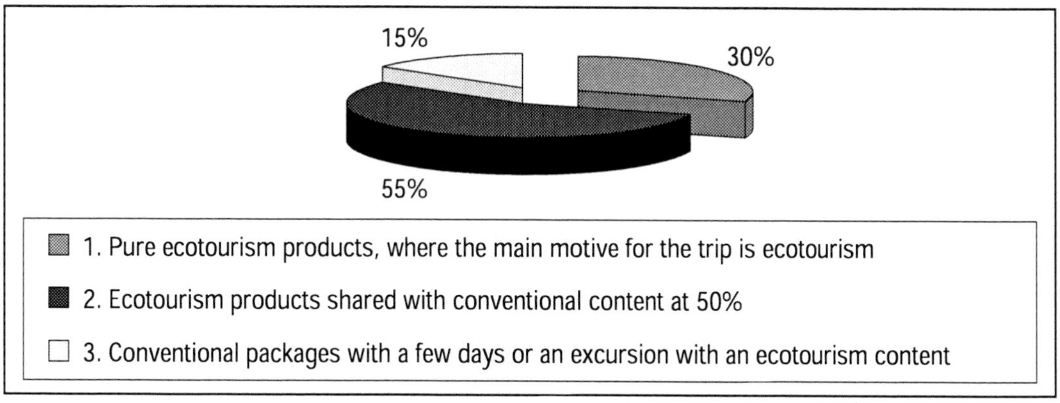

TO Survey (N=27), Planta 2001

On these trips or ecotourism packages which are organized by the tour operators, what is valued above all, is respect for the natural environment and that the groups of tourists are small.

Diagram 9. Important aspects of ecotourism packages

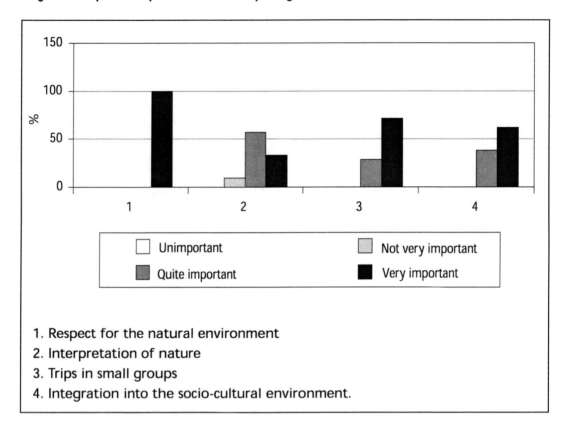

1. Respect for the natural environment
2. Interpretation of nature
3. Trips in small groups
4. Integration into the socio-cultural environment.

TO Survey(N=21), Planta 2001

The themes or activities included in the ecotourism packages are, as diagram 10 illustrates, many and very varied. We can highlight the following: observation of fauna, nature trekking, visits to protected areas and coexistence with indigenous and traditional communities. On a second level we would find: exploration trails, sport trekking, trips of naturalist interest, natural /cultural heritage, ethnology, etc.

Diagram 10. Activities included in ecotourism products

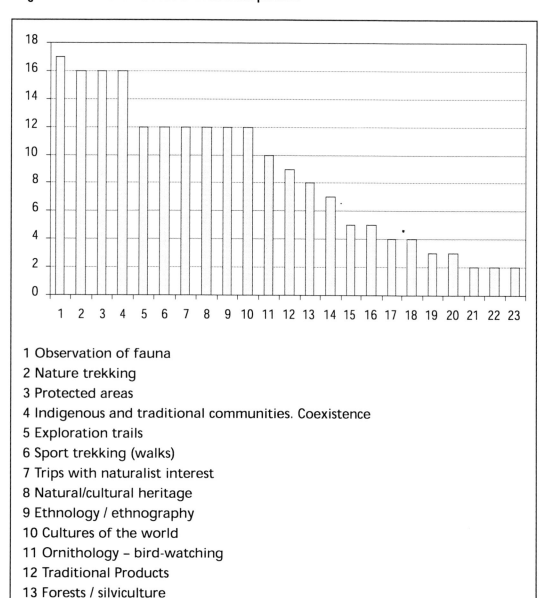

1 Observation of fauna
2 Nature trekking
3 Protected areas
4 Indigenous and traditional communities. Coexistence
5 Exploration trails
6 Sport trekking (walks)
7 Trips with naturalist interest
8 Natural/cultural heritage
9 Ethnology / ethnography
10 Cultures of the world
11 Ornithology – bird-watching
12 Traditional Products
13 Forests / silviculture
14 Vulcanology
15 Geology / palaeontology
16 Astronomy
17 Sustainable hunting/fishing
18 Support for and collaboration with conservation programmes
19 Learning local techniques
20 Others
21 Botanical, medicinal plant walks
22 Scientific research, study trips
23 Eco-volunteering

TO Survey (N=27), Planta 2001

Duration of ecotourism trips / packages

The duration of the ecotourism trips organized by the TOs is generally between two and three weeks for destinations outside Europe, two weeks for destinations inside Europe and one week for destinations in Spain (Diagram 11). We can find some differences between this data and the duration of the ecotourism trips as manifested by the people surveyed in FITUR (Diagram 12), nevertheless, they are not important differences and are caused by the trips which are organized personally or directly by the tourists without going through an agency or tour operators.

Diagram 11. Average duration of the ecotourism trips-packages programmed by the tour operators

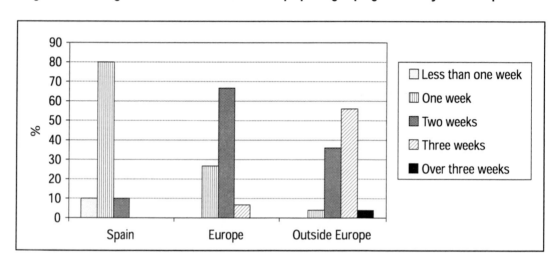

TO Survey (N=25), Planta 2001

Diagram 12. Average duration of the trips made by ecotourists

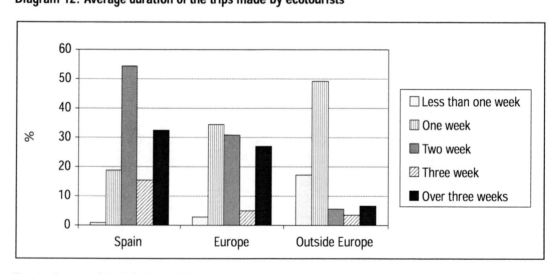

Tourist Surveys (N=424), Fitur 2001

Seasonal variation

The ecotourism market suffers the same problems of high seasonal variation as the Spanish conventional tourism market; as can be seen in the analysis of the interviews with operators, the majority of ecotourism packages are sold in summer.

Diagram 13. Seasonal variation of the ecotourism trips / packages programmed by the tour operators

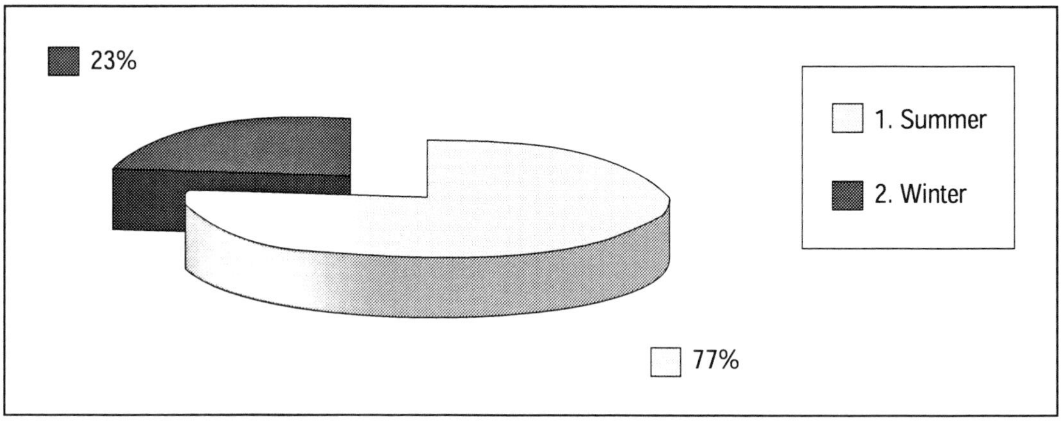

TO Survey, Planta 2001

3.5. Main ecotourism destinations

Rural tourism has traditionally been defined as inland tourism, in which the destinations are not situated at a great distance from the point of origin. Nevertheless, when we talk about ecotourism, the distances are greatly enlarged, with the main ecotourism destinations being situated outside Europe.

Destinations offered by the tour operators

As regards what is offered, all the world regions are represented to a greater or lesser extent in the programmes proposed by the Spanish ecotourism tour operators. (diagram 14). With respect to Tourist Offices operating in Spain, 73 countries have tourist offices in Madrid, Barcelona or another city, providing information, prospectus, maps. etc. to those who make requests by telephone. Fax, E-mail as well as attending to visits in their offices. Nature and ecotourism destinations as important as the following do not have a tourist office in Spain, which indicates the relative importance of the Spanish outbound ecotourism market: Namibia, Tanzania, Malawi, Mongolia, New Zealand, Russia, Surinam, Vietnam, Yemen, Zambia, Zimbabwe, Botswana, Tahiti, etc.

Diagram 14. Geographical areas offered by the tour operators

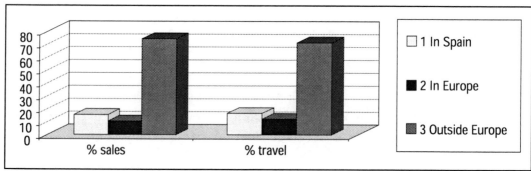

TO Survey, Planta 2001

The majority of ecotourism sales and trips are made outside Europe (74% of sales and 71% of trips), with an important difference between trips and sales in Spain and Europe.

**Diagram 15. Distribution of sales/trips among the Spanish,
European and non-European destinations**

TO Survey, Planta 2001

Latin America and Africa, in particular Namibia, Tanzania and Botswana in Africa, and Guatemala, Peru and Argentina in Latin America stand out as the most common destinations. As for Europe, Spain, Scandinavia and almost Spain's neighbouring countries feature prominently.

Destinations preferred by ecotourists

From the point of view of demand, the majority of tourists also prefer distant countries outside Europe for trips of an ecotourist nature (42% of the total), nevertheless, Europe, and Spain to be precise, are also chosen by a high percentage of tour operators' clients (Diagram 17).

Diagram 16. Geographical areas preferred by tourists (FITUR) for trips of an ecotourism nature

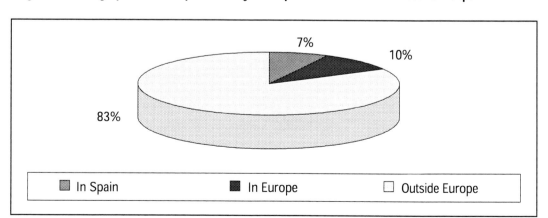

31.6%   41.7%

26.8%

■ 1. Distant, exotic countries   ■ 2. European countries   □ 3. Spanish destinations

Tourist Surveys (N=424), FITUR 2001

A breakdown of each area (distant, European and Spanish destinations) can be found in Annex 7.

Once again we find differences between the data obtained through interviews with operators and that obtained in surveys of tourists, this is due to the operators being contacted by ecotourism clients mainly for trips outside Spain.

Diagram 17. Geographical areas preferred by tour operator's clients for ecotourism trips

7%   10%

83%

■ In Spain   ■ In Europe   □ Outside Europe

TO Survey, Planta 2001

Among the destinations abroad, a clear preference can be seen for Latin American and African countries, with Brazil and Argentina featuring prominently, followed by Mexico and Cuba. Other destinations very much in demand are in Asia, such as India and Nepal. Countries such as Australia or Egypt are also chosen by a significant percentage of ecotourists.

In Europe, the following destinations stand out: Italy, the Scandinavian and Nordic countries, France, Great Britain, The Alps and Greece.

As for domestic tourism, within Spain 38% of tourists surveyed prefer destinations in the North of Spain, "Green Spain" (Asturias, Galicia, Basque Country, Cantabria, etc.), or to visit National Parks (principally Doñana, Ordesa and Picos de Europa National parks), although the islands (especially the Canaries) and Andalusia are also highly valued.

Table 2. Geographical areas preferred by tour operator's clients for ecotourism trips

SPAIN:	%
National Parks	26.7
Andalusia	13.3
Asturias	13.3
Galicia	13.3
Pyrenees	13.3
Canary Islands	6.7
Sierra	6.7
Coast	6.7
Total Responses	**100.0**

EUROPE:	%
Alps	26.3
Scandinavia	26.3
Nordic Countries	15.8
Portugal	10.5
United Kingdom	10.5
Bulgaria	5.3
Iceland	5.3
Romania	5.3
TOTAL Responses	**100**

OUTSIDE EUROPE:	%
Africa	23.53
Latin America	22.06
Asia	17.65
North America	10.29
Middle East	10.29
Oceania	8.82
Caribbean	7.35
Total	**100.00**

TO Survey, Planta 2001

3.6. Conclusion

In conclusion, it can be said that the Spanish ecotourism market, although still small, and subject to problems of seasonal variation, is an emerging market with potential and whose demand for ecotourism products and destinations will gradually increase.

As regards what Spanish tour operators and travel agents offer, we can see that it has increased rapidly in recent years, and it is anticipated that it will continue to do so, responding to the increase in demand.

IV. Typology and Attitude of the Ecotourism Consumers

4.1. Profile and socio-demographic aspects of the ecotourism consumer

The consumer of ecotourism trips / packages, or the ecotourist, can be situated within a specific profile based on their socio-demographic characteristics.

Socio-demographic category of the ecotourist

The Spanish outbound tourist market is, in comparison with that of other outbound tourism countries with a longer tradition of tourism and travel, relatively young. Apart from the social and economic elite which has always travelled abroad, in Spain, generalized trips abroad are, for a large section of society, a relatively recent phenomenon. The global outbound tourism market is therefore a young market. In this context, ecotourism trips are even more recent. This is confirmed by the fact that the age group that goes on most ecotourism-type trips is that of 20 to 39 years of age, followed by the 40 to 59 year-old group. The over 60 age group is hardly represented.

Diagram 18. Average age of the ecotourist client

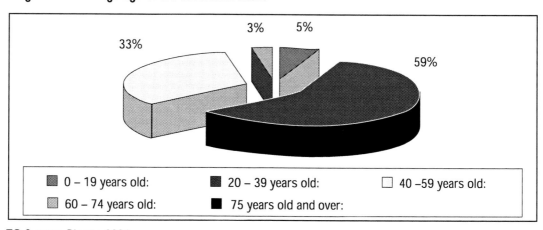

33%   3%   5%   59%

▦ 0 – 19 years old:	■ 20 – 39 years old:	☐ 40 –59 years old:
▨ 60 – 74 years old:	■ 75 years old and over:	

TO Survey, Planta 2001

As regards the sex of the ecotourist, women in general make up the group which travels most, 55% as opposed to 45% of men. This proportion is only inverted in the toughest packages with trekking, exploration, etc.

Diagram 19. The Sex of the ecotourist

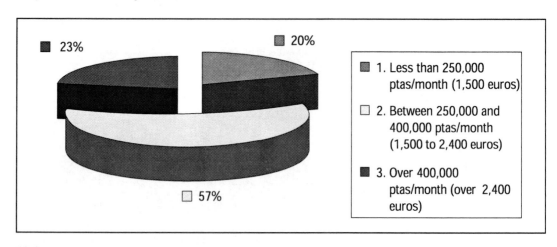

TO Survey, Planta 2001

Socio-economic category of the ecotourist

The population group that goes on most ecotourism trips organized by tour operators earns between 250,000 and 400,000 pesetas per month, which is about 1,500-2,400 euros/month (Diagram 20). The groups that earn more and less than these amounts are relatively equal. Whereas, from the point of view of demand, the population group which responds best to the ecotourism market earns less than 250,000 pesetas (1,500 euros) per month, that is more coherent with the average age group to which they belong. These figures should be kept in mind in relation to the average Spanish salary, which is approximately 185,000 ptas./month (1,112 €/month)

Diagram 20. Net Salary/month

■ 23%   ■ 20%

■ 1. Less than 250,000 ptas/month (1,500 euros)

□ 2. Between 250,000 and 400,000 ptas/month (1,500 to 2,400 euros)

■ 3. Over 400,000 ptas/month (over 2,400 euros)

□ 57%

TO Survey, Planta 2001

As far as the level of education is concerned, the majority of ecotourists belong to higher categories and have received a university education.

Diagram 21. Education / social category

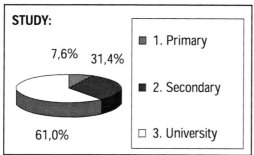

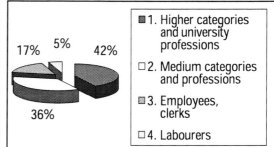

Tourist Surveys (N=424), Fitu 2001   TO Survey, Planta 2001

Geographical origin of the ecotourist

The majority of the tour operators' clients interviewed came from Madrid and Barcelona, and the Basque Country is also represented, but these data correspond to the cities in which the surveyed entities are located. As regards demand, Madrid Region features prominently as the place of origin for the typical ecotourist, which in itself is not significant given that the survey was carried out in the city, nevertheless, Valencia Region and Andalusia also have an important representation. It is not possible to determine whether the Spanish ecotourist lives only in the big cities, or if the inhabitants of provincial capitals and rural areas also answer to the description of ecotourists.

Diagram 22. Geographical origin

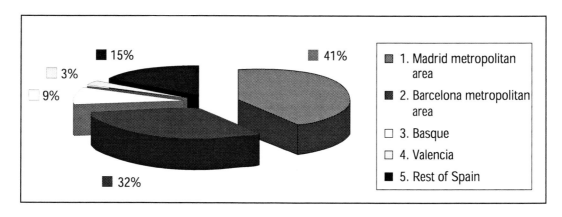

TO Survey, Planta 2001

Organization of the trip, reservations, dates, etc.

Depending on how the trip is organized, the way reservations are made, the choice of date, etc. we could also define the typical ecotourist. Thanks to the tour operators interviewed, it is calculated that approximately 65% of the ecotourists who plan a trip to a destination that is programmed by operators, prepare their trips through travel agencies or tour operators, the remaining 35% prepare their trips independently. Whereas, if we consider the data extracted from the tourist surveys, only 40% of those surveyed admitted to always or preferably planning their trips through agencies (Table 3). These figures, therefore, are not conclusive, because we should also keep in mind the distance to the destination and the "degree of difficulty" as regards language, information and available guides, maps, flights from Spain, etc. For destinations in Spain or Europe it is easier to plan trips independently.

Table 3.Reservation of ecotourism trips

RESERVATION OF TRIPS:	Always	Preferably	Sometimes	TOTAL percentages·
Personally/ Directly	25.15%	18.66%	7.10%	50.91%
Through travel agency / operator	25.15%	14.81%	9.13%	49.09%

* Although the results are similar, the surveyed population shows a tendency to reserve trips to destinations within Spain personally, and trips abroad through an agency.

Tourist Surveys (N=424), FITUR 2001

The authors of this study, due to their experience in work with the tourist offices of Bolivia, Nicaragua, Peru and some African countries, consider that a distribution of between 25% and 30% through outbound operators in Spain and between 65-70% of independent trips, a large number of which acquire the services of a receiving agency upon arrival at the destination, is due to the rapid growth of the Spanish adventure tourism and ecotourism market.

As regards the preferred dates, as was confirmed by analysis of the interviews and surveys, 77% of trips take place in summer, according to the operators, and 60% of the tourists surveyed expressed a preference for travelling in summer, mainly in the month of August. (diagram 23). Nevertheless, as was pointed out earlier, this tendency is slowly changing in favour of greater variation in the seasonal nature of tourism.

Diagram 23. Date when trips take place

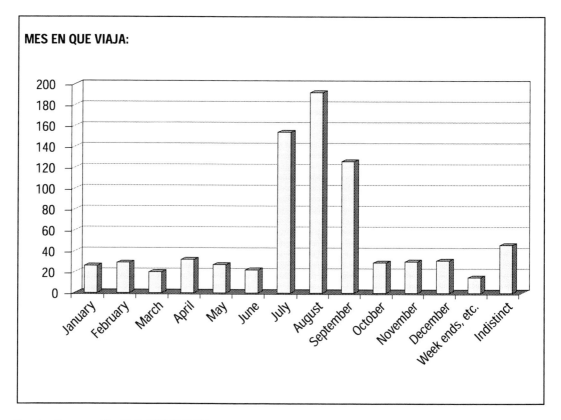

MES EN QUE VIAJA:

Tourist Surveys (N=424), FITUR 2001

4.2. Ecotourists' motives and requirements

As mentioned earlier, the majority of tourists distribute their time equally between nature activities and other types of activities ("mixed" ecotourism packages); only 17% of those surveyed devote the maximum amount of time available to the observation of wild fauna and the enjoyment of the natural landscape, both of which would be genuine ecotourism activities.

Main motives of the ecotourist consumer

According to the data extracted from the tourist surveys in Fitur and interviews with operators, we can conclude that, among the clients that resort to an operator or travel agency to organize an ecotourism trip or nature trip, the main reason is the participation in certain activities traditionally offered by ecotourism, among which visits to protected areas or Nature Reserves feature prominently. This is mainly due to the fact these natural areas are perceived by consumers as having aspects or attractions essential to an ecotourism destination, such as the chance to practise certain activities in direct contact with nature, the observation of flora and fauna, the presence of relatively unspoiled landscapes, etc.

Other ecotourism motives are equally important when choosing a trip of this type, such as coexistence with indigenous populations and the contemplation of exceptional fauna and landscapes.

Diagram 24. Motives of tour operators' ecotourism clients for going on nature trips

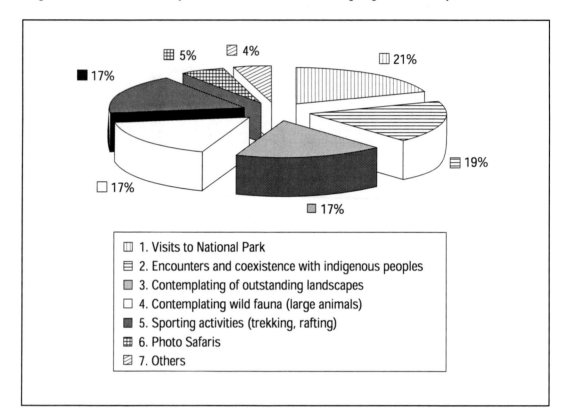

TO Survey, Planta 2001

Requirements of tourist destinations / packages

The following diagram includes the fundamental characteristics or aspects which an ecotourism destination should have. The following aspects stand out: artistic-cultural (18% of the responses), nature (17.5%), different cultures and traditions (17%) and landscape (15%).

Diagram 25. Characteristics which make a destination attractive

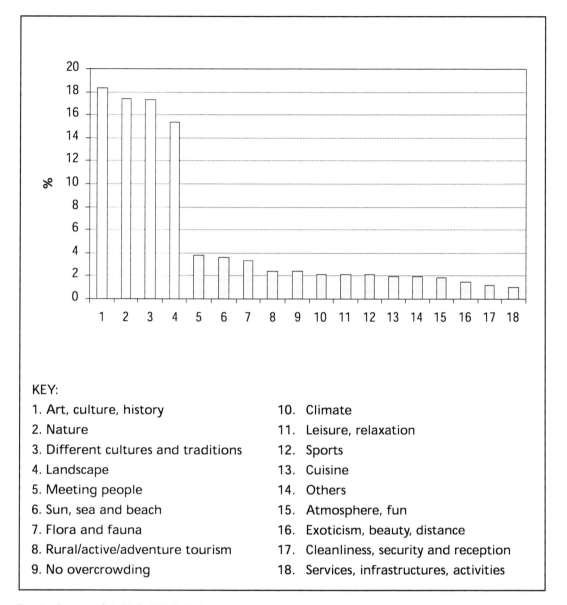

KEY:
1. Art, culture, history
2. Nature
3. Different cultures and traditions
4. Landscape
5. Meeting people
6. Sun, sea and beach
7. Flora and fauna
8. Rural/active/adventure tourism
9. No overcrowding

10. Climate
11. Leisure, relaxation
12. Sports
13. Cuisine
14. Others
15. Atmosphere, fun
16. Exoticism, beauty, distance
17. Cleanliness, security and reception
18. Services, infrastructures, activities

Tourist Surveys (N=424), FITUR 2001

Apart from the above aspects, there are other important requirements for the ecotourism client, related to what is on offer locally at the destination, what the ecotourism package / destination should contain in order to be finally chosen by the consumer. These demands are referred to in the following diagram.

Diagram 26. Most important aspects (requirements) for consumers in an ecotourism destination

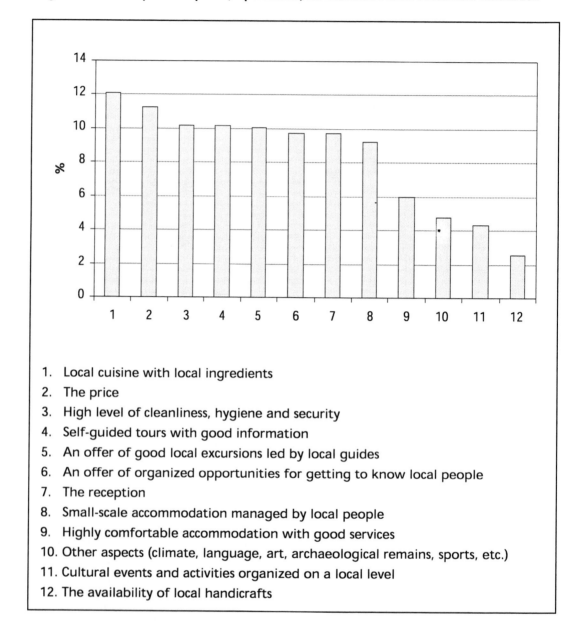

1. Local cuisine with local ingredients
2. The price
3. High level of cleanliness, hygiene and security
4. Self-guided tours with good information
5. An offer of good local excursions led by local guides
6. An offer of organized opportunities for getting to know local people
7. The reception
8. Small-scale accommodation managed by local people
9. Highly comfortable accommodation with good services
10. Other aspects (climate, language, art, archaeological remains, sports, etc.)
11. Cultural events and activities organized on a local level
12. The availability of local handicrafts

Tourist Surveys (N=424), Fitur 2001

However, the existence of a percentage of tourists who do not know or are not sure what the most important aspects of an ecotourism destination are for them, perhaps due to the lack of consensus as regards its definition, as a lack of unity regarding what ecotourism really means can also be appreciated. Many people relate ecotourism simply with visits to protected areas. Thus, a certain lack of motivational definition exists, which is still very generic compared with that of other countries.

4.3. Ecotourism activities

The introduction of experiences of direct contact with nature and visits to National Parks / nature reserves or protected areas into the tourism market, has led to these activities becoming highly valued by the ecotourists when it comes to choosing the ecotourism destination / package. (diagrams 27 and 28).

Diagram 27. The offer of experiences of direct contact with nature is important when it comes to choosing the destination. *

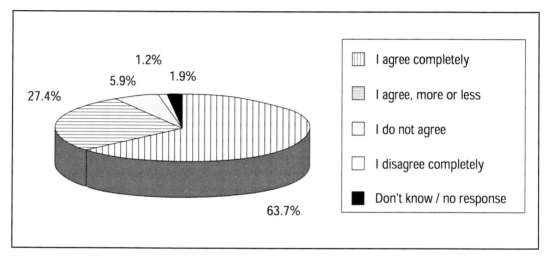

Tourist Surveys (N=424), Fitur 2001

Diagram 28. The visit to a National Park / nature reserve or protected area is important when it comes to choosing the destination *

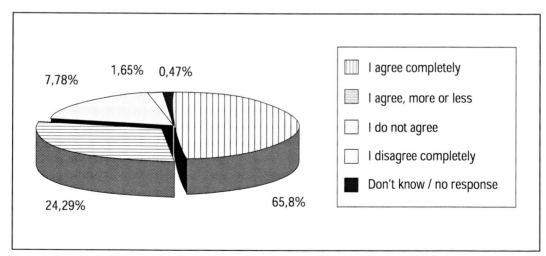

Tourist Surveys (N=424), Fitur 2001

---

* Data extracted from Diagram 31

Diagram 29 shows the main ecotourism activities which take place on trips according to the tourists surveyed in FITUR. The most popular activity on ecotourism trips is a visit to protected areas (29% of those surveyed have made a visit to protected areas as their main ecotourism activity). Other activities are also in demand, such as trekking (13%) and the contemplation of fauna (5%), followed by certain nature sports or a combination of diverse activities (adventure, protected areas, sports, etc.).

Diagram 29. Main activity on ecotourism trips

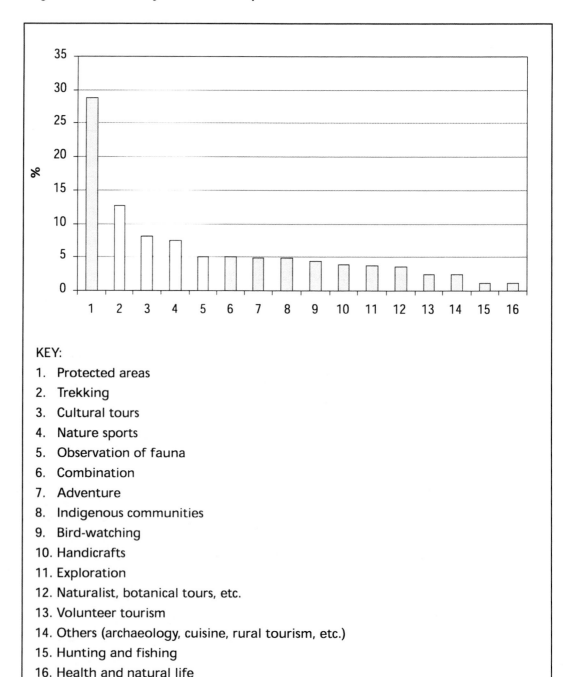

KEY:
1. Protected areas
2. Trekking
3. Cultural tours
4. Nature sports
5. Observation of fauna
6. Combination
7. Adventure
8. Indigenous communities
9. Bird-watching
10. Handicrafts
11. Exploration
12. Naturalist, botanical tours, etc.
13. Volunteer tourism
14. Others (archaeology, cuisine, rural tourism, etc.)
15. Hunting and fishing
16. Health and natural life

Tourist Surveys (N=424), Fitur 2001

A breakdown of each activity according to destination can be found in Annex 6.

4.4. Ecotourist behaviour and awareness

Classification of the ecotourist according to behaviour

For the tour operators, the decisive factors in classifying a client as an ecotourist are the choice of an exploration, nature product etc. (30%) and selection of a clearly ecotourist destination (28%). Nevertheless, these aspects do not give us any information about the real behaviour of the tourist at the destination. (Diagram 30). Another type of decisive behaviour is a request for highly detailed information about the destination (28%), although this information may have nothing to do with environmental aspects, due to the fact that the ecotourist usually gathers this information himself/herself.

Diagram 30. Decisive behaviour for classifying a client of a tour operators as an ecotourist

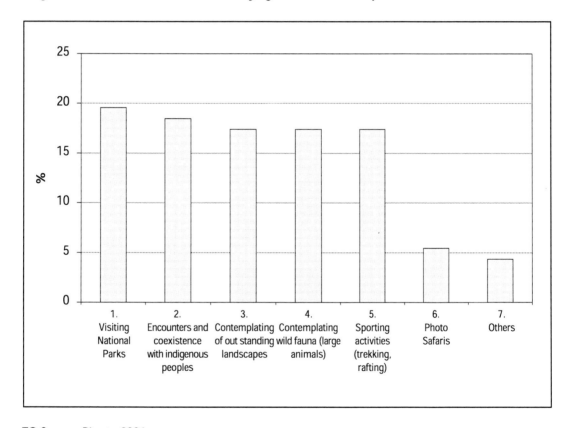

TO Survey, Planta 2001

The financial or voluntary contribution of the Spanish tourist to the destination communities is virtually non-existent.

Level of awareness of conservation issues and the socio-cultural and environmental implications of ecotourism

Respect for the local culture and traditions is one of the most important aspects for the great majority of ecotourists (85%). The conservation of nature and landscape is equally important, a preserved environment makes their holidays more satisfactory and they are horrified by landscapes which have been destroyed by urban and infrastructure excesses (Diagram 31).

Diagram 31. Level of agreement with the following ecotourism issues:

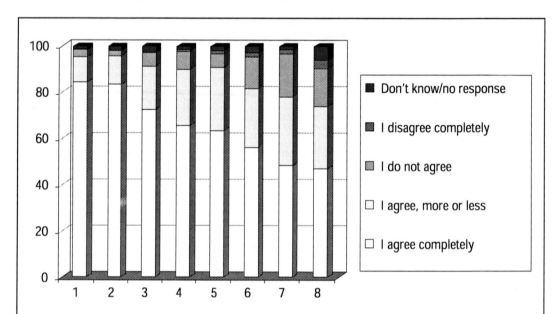

KEY:

1. Respect for the local traditions and way of life is very important.
2. A well-preserved environment is very important if my holidays are to be satisfactory
3. I find tourist destinations with landscapes spoilt by urban and infrastructure excesses very off-putting.
4. The visit to a National Park / nature reserve or protected area is important when it comes to choosing the destination
5. The offer of experiences of direct contact with nature is important when it comes to choosing the destination.
6. I expect the travel agencies to provide me with good information about the environmental aspects of the tourist destination.
7. The observation of wild fauna is important when it comes to choosing the destination.
8. The operator's (agent's) environmental commitment to the destination is important when if comes to choosing an operator-programme-agent.

Tourist Surveys (N=424), FITUR 2001

Fewer than half of the tourists surveyed thought that the operator's commitment to the environment was important when choosing an operator-programme-agent. Even a significant percentage disagreed with this affirmation. This may indicate a lack of awareness on the part of the tourist. Besides, although tourists declare a preference for well-conserved nature and landscape, this does not mean that they behave in a respectable manner towards the environment.

4.5. Conclusion

Based on the socio-demographic and economic characteristics of the ecotourist clients analyzed earlier, we can obtain a particular profile;

- The typical ecotourist is between 20-39 years old,
- is usually a woman, especially on "soft" ecotourism packages,
- his salary varies between 250,000 and 400,000 ptas./month (1,500 – 2,400 €),
- has received a university education and/or has higher professional positions,
- comes from different geographical areas, mainly metropolitan areas,
- For the most part, prepares his trips through tour operators or travel agents, especially for destinations abroad, and
- makes the trips during the summer months.

As regards the motives for the ecotourism trip, visits to protected and natural areas feature prominently, as do the possibilities of taking part in activities in direct contact with nature, coexistence with other cultures and the contemplation of flora and fauna and outstanding or relatively unspoilt landscapes.

V. Marketing Channels and Tour Operators' Attitudes

5.1. Tour operators' and tourist offices' opinion and use of the term Ecotourism.

Agreement with the definition of Ecotourism

The majority of the tour operator managers interviewed more or less agree, or agree completely with the WTO definition of ecotourism (Diagram 32). If they are not in complete agreement, it is because Spain has been using another definition or because the terms (ecotourism, nature or adventure tourism, etc.) are mixed up. They do not identify with the term ecotourism which is alien to them and they consider it to be too general and ambiguous, rhetorical, frequently used without rigour, in an unclear and unprofessional manner, etc.

Diagram 32. Do you agree with the WTO's definition of the term 'ecotourism'?

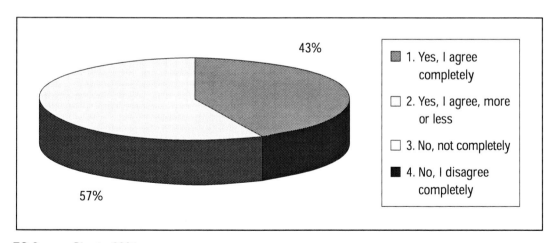

43%

57%

1. Yes, I agree completely
2. Yes, I agree, more or less
3. No, not completely
4. No, I disagree completely

TO Survey, Planta 2001

Use of the term Ecotourism

Only 52.3% of tour operators and Offices use the term ecotourism in the promotion of their products, although the majority believe that it is a concept with a future, but which has not yet been well-implanted in Spain. Nature tourism, green tourism, active tourism, adventure tourism, alternative tourism, expeditions, trekking, multi-adventure, exploration trails.... these terms, more technical and precise, are more common in the Spanish operators' and agencies' catalogues. It is symptomatic that the main association of Spanish operators and agencies that offer ecotourism products is called "Independent Association of Adventure Travel Agencies".

Diagram 33. Do you use the term ecotourism to promote your company or products?

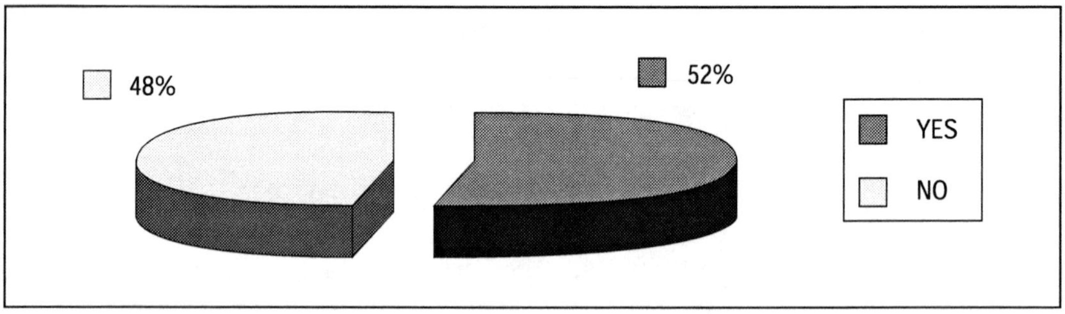

48%   52%

YES

NO

TO Survey, Planta 2001

The Spanish Ecotourism Society, the only entity which uses the term "ecotourism" in the Spanish context, was created recently by a group of professionals, and has not yet been able to have a significant demonstration effect in helping the term "catch on" in the sector and in society. Moreover, it has not been able to count on significant participation, as members, from the commercial or tourist distribution sector -agencies and operators-, or from suppliers and providers- hotels, country houses, multi-activity companies, etc.-.

Development and Positioning of the Ecotourism concept

Despite the lack of agreement in the definition of ecotourism or its relative use among operators and travel agents, 90% of the tour operators interviewed were of the opinion that the concept had a future, and 90% were also in favour of developing it among Spanish travel agents.

Among the different methods of positioning the concept of ecotourism in the Spanish market and developing it, the tour operators interviewed were in favour of organizing a national awareness campaign about ecotourism, as well as distributing a code of ethical behaviour among tourists.

Diagram 34. Methods for developing and positioning the concept of ecotourism in the Spanish market

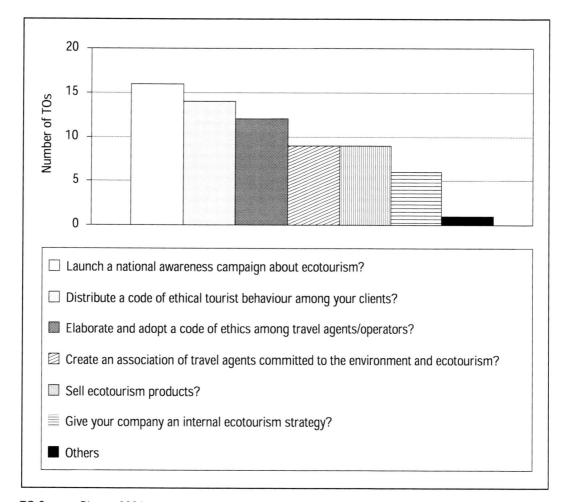

TO Survey, Planta 2001

5.2. The role of the tour operators and tourist offices

Travel agents and tour operators are commonly used media for the organization of ecotourism trips abroad or for buying certain predesigned packages.

As mentioned earlier, approximately half the people surveyed reserve these ecotourism-type trips personally or directly and the other half use agencies. Nevertheless, we can observe a clear tendency towards reserving and organizing trips to destinations within Spain personally, and going through an agency or tour operator for the more difficult destinations abroad.

Supplying services

With respect to the services that clients expect from tour operators, although many would like the travel agencies to provide them with good information about the environmental aspects of the tourist destination, a significant percentage do not agree, do not consider it important or do not expect the agency to provide the information, and they gather it by themselves (Diagram 35).

Diagram 35. I expect the travel agencies to provide me with good information about the environmental aspects of the tourist destination.. *

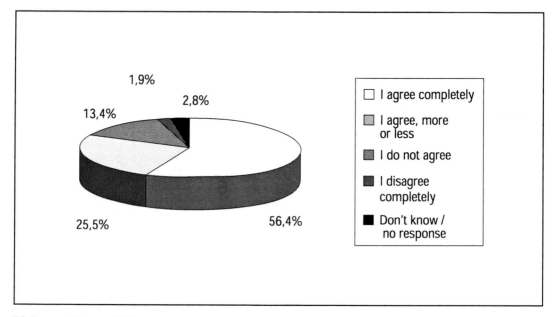

1,9%
2,8%
13,4%
25,5%
56,4%

- ☐ I agree completely
- I agree, more or less
- I do not agree
- I disagree completely
- ■ Don't know / no response

TO Survey, Planta 2001

With regard to other types of data which agencies or operators place at their clients disposal, it is worth pointing out that the majority of tour operators offer an information dossier prior to the trip (Diagram 36). It is also common to hold meetings prior to the commencement of the trip; however, Spanish operators hardly offer any information about conservation programmes, about endangered flora and fauna or a manual of good practices, (this situation may be due to the destinations not always being consolidated, low passenger volume, lack of demand on the part of the travellers in this respect).

* Data extracted from Diagram 31

Diagram 36. Information available to ecotourism clients

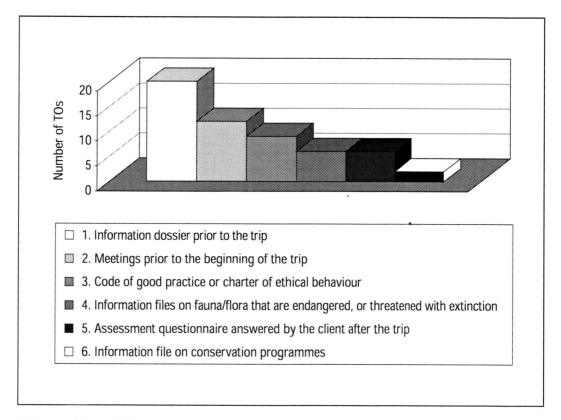

TO Survey, Planta 2001

A monitoring of the ecotourism client after the trip by means of travel assessment questionnaires, or any other means, is not usual either.

5.3. Main promotion channels

Apart from the traditional "sale" of tourist products through the catalogue, as observed in diagram 37, what is known as "word of mouth" is the main form of transmission of tour operators offers or products. This phenomenon, despite being beyond their control, is one of the best tools to spread information in Spain. Another of the main forms of promotion is presenting the most attractive products on the Internet, or by appearing at trade fairs and shows which specialize in ecotourism.

Diagram 37. Methods of providing information about/promoting ecotourism products

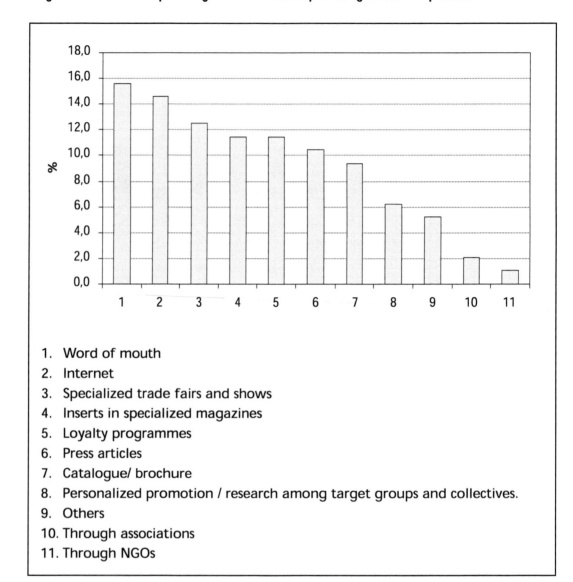

1. Word of mouth
2. Internet
3. Specialized trade fairs and shows
4. Inserts in specialized magazines
5. Loyalty programmes
6. Press articles
7. Catalogue/ brochure
8. Personalized promotion / research among target groups and collectives.
9. Others
10. Through associations
11. Through NGOs

TO Survey, Planta 2001

Television and Radio are other technologies used for the promotion of a tour operator or its products, as well as the holding of chats and slide shows and Fam trips (destination familiarization trips, where the operators are invited to learn more about the destination they offer and sell).

Virtually all the tour operators publish a catalogue or brochure with the products differentiated by type, destination or predominant tourist activity.

The Tourist Offices also possess exclusive catalogues for ecotourism products, and some of them organize familiarization trips for specialized tour operators.

5.4. Conclusion

As it was mentioned earlier, total agreement among tour operators regarding the WTO's concrete definition of ecotourism does not exist. And, therefore, it is not used as much as it could be in their tourism offers. This lack of consensus is mainly due to the diversity of similar terms which have traditionally been used in Spain, such as rural, adventure, nature tourism, alternative tourism, sustainable tourism, etc.

Nevertheless, the tour operators are of the opinion that ecotourism has a healthy future, and are in favour of developing it among Spanish travel agents and tour operators.

Almost half of the ecotourists surveyed use travel agencies and tour operators to programme and carry out their trips, especially for destinations abroad. This data is an important indicator of the fundamental role of the TOs in the ecotourism market.

Tour operators have an important role with regard to the ecotourism destination, programming the trips in such a way so as to respect environmental and cultural values, as well as creating employment in said destinations.

The tour operators' relationship with the destination and the ecology

As far as the relationship between operators and tourist destinations is concerned, we can conclude that they are mainly guided by the principle of respect for the environment, and therefore organize trips in small groups. These aspects are very important for tour operators and tourist offices, nevertheless, this is not the case with the interpretation of nature or the integration into the socio-cultural environment (diagram 38).

Diagram 38. Importance of the following aspects

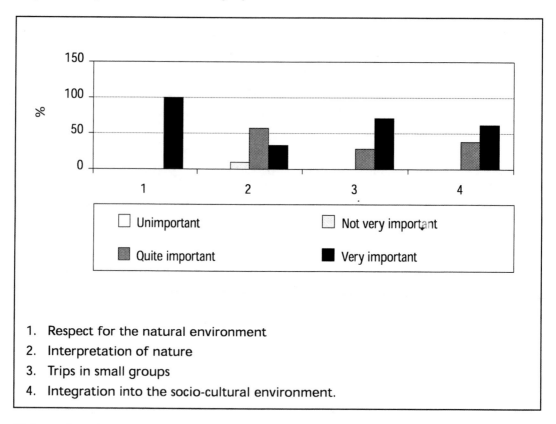

1. Respect for the natural environment
2. Interpretation of nature
3. Trips in small groups
4. Integration into the socio-cultural environment.

TO Survey(N=21), Planta 2001

Commitment to ecological issues

As can be seen from the following diagrams, the overwhelming majority of tour operators do not finance, or participate directly in local environmental protection or protected area projects (78% and 82% respectively). Neither do they use voluntary co-operation as a marketing tool to create a particular image, due to the fact that they would consider it unethical behaviour. Nevertheless, a small percentage of tour operators are members of associations that do protect nature, such as Greenpeace or WWF/ADENA.

Diagram 39. Does your company finance or participate in local environmental protection programmes?

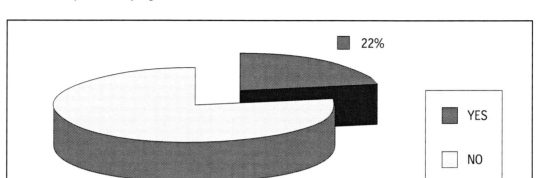

Diagram 40. Does your company participate or involve itself in collaboration/co-operation action regarding protected areas?

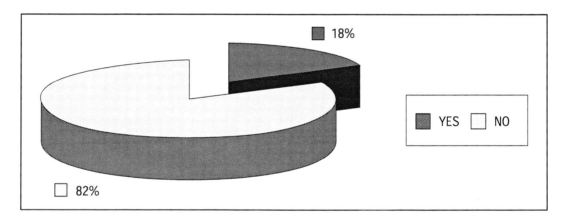

Only 33% of tour operators encourage their clients to make donations to conservation or local development projects and they do so by means of free publicity, orally, etc. (diagram 41). However, they themselves do favour employing local suppliers (diagram 42).

Diagram 41. Do you encourage your clients to make donations to local conservation and development projects?

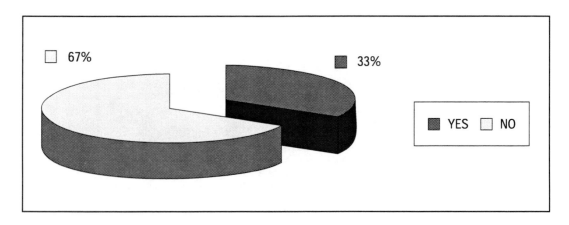

Diagram 42. Does your company favour the use of local providers/suppliers?

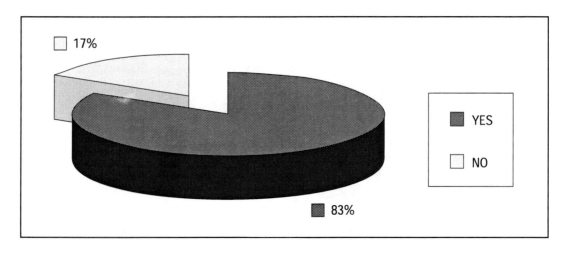

Besides, 72% of the tour operators interviewed would be prepared to invest in favour of local suppliers or providers, advising them on the setting up of their products, improving their features and including their products in their company's brochure or assuming the role of advisor and partner in the production and commercialization of ecotourism products.

Diagram 43. Would your company be prepared to invest in favour of your local suppliers/providers? How?

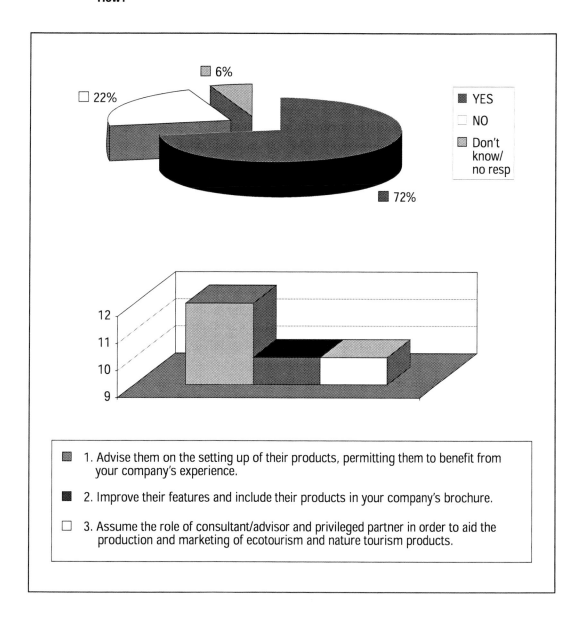

1. Advise them on the setting up of their products, permitting them to benefit from your company's experience.

2. Improve their features and include their products in your company's brochure.

3. Assume the role of consultant/advisor and privileged partner in order to aid the production and marketing of ecotourism and nature tourism products.

Annexes

Annex 1: Model of survey for visitors to the Spanish ecotourism market

Annex 2: Model of survey / interview with specialized operators and agencies

Annex 3: List of tour operators contacted

Annex 4: Analysis of brochures / catalogues

Annex 5: PICTE Survey: Spanish tourists' stays.

Annex 6: Breakdown of question 4 of the tourist survey:
Have you made? Any ecotourism trip in the past?

Annex 7: Breakdown of question 5 of the tourist survey:
Which destinations interest you most for this type of trip?

Annex 8: Québec Declaration on Ecotourism

Annex 1
Model of Survey

MODEL OF SURVEY FOR VISITORS TO THE SPANISH ECOTOURISM MARKET

The year 2002 will be "International Year of Ecotourism". The World Tourism Organization (WTO) is carrying out a study about the ecotourism market in 4 European countries and we (Planta, S.A.) have been commissioned to do it in Spain.

Could you collaborate by devoting a few minutes to answering several brief questions?

FITUR 2001

| INTERVIEWER: |
| DAY: TIME: |

1. On your last main holiday, what were the two main motives / reasons for choosing the destination?

		1st motive	2nd motive
1.	Enjoy sun, sea and beach		
2.	Rest, relax		
3.	Have fun with friends		
4.	Learn about other cultures		
5.	Contemplate other landscapes and get a change of scenery		
6.	Observe wild fauna and enjoy nature		
7.	Get to know and contact indigenous cultures		
8.	Experience adventures in areas of unspoiled nature		
9.	Spend time with the family		
10.	Others		
11.	Don't know		
12.	No response		

2. If 5, 6, 7 or 8 were the 1st or 2nd motive, what for you were the 3 most important aspects (requirements) of a travel destination:

- Small-scale accommodation managed by local people
- Highly comfortable accommodation with good services
- Local cuisine with local ingredients
- High level of cleanliness, hygiene and security
- An offer of good local excursions led by local guides
- elf-guided tours with good information
- An offer of organized opportunities for getting to know local people
- Cultural events and activities organized on a local level
- The availability of local handicrafts
- The reception
- The price
- Other aspects such as...
- Don't know
- No response

3. The following question is more specifically about nature and the environment. Do you agree completely, more or less, disagree or disagree completely with the following opinions?

	I agree completely	I agree, more or less	I disagree	I disagree completely
• A well-preserved environment is very important if my holidays are to be satisfactory				
• Respect for the local traditions and way of life is very important.				
• Tourist destinations with landscapes spoilt by urban and infrastructure excesses horrify me.				
• I expect the travel agencies to provide me with good information about the environmental aspects of the tourist destination.				
• The operator's (agent's) environmental commitment to the destination is important when if comes to choosing an operator-programme-agent.				
• The offer of experiences of direct contact with nature is important when it comes to choosing the destination.				
• The observation of wild fauna is important when it comes to choosing the destination.				
• The visit to a National Park / nature reserve or protected area is important when it comes to choosing the destination				

4. Although experiencing contact with nature, the observation of wild fauna and/or visits to nature reserves / national parks, were not your main motive for choosing a holiday destination, have you been on these types of trips in the past?

❏ Yes, regularly   ❏ Yes, but only once
❏ Yes, from time to time   ❏ No

If so, what type of trips were they. Indicate the main activity:

❏ Visits to national parks/protected areas in:	❏ Observation of fauna in:
❏ Bird-watching in:	❏ Trekking:
❏ Exploration trails in:	❏ Other nature sports. Diving, horses, etc. in:
❏ Naturalist, botanical, medicinal plant, geology, trips etc. in:	❏ Adventure, multi-adventure in: ❏ Cultural trips (cultures of the world) in:
❏ Life/stays with indigenous communities and learning about traditions, local culture:	❏ Handicrafts ❏ Health and natural life:
❏ Solidarity Tourism/voluntary work, training in:	❏ Sustainable hunting and fishing
❏ Combination of the above aspects: Please specify:	❏ Other themes. Please specify

If you have never been on a trip of this type, please explain, briefly, why not? (reasons): ....
....

5. Which destinations interest you most for this type of trip?

❏ Above all, I am interested in trips to distant and exotic countries.
Destinations:

❏ Above all, I am interested in stays of this type in other European countries.
Destinations:

❏ My favourite destinations of this type are in Spain.
Destinations:

6. What characteristics / aspects of those destinations make them particularly attractive for you?

_____

7. How many days do these trips usually last:

❏ Long distance: ❏ European Destinations: ❏ Spain:

8. How do you reserve these trips:

	Always	Preferably	Sometimes	Never
❏ Personally / Directly ❏ Through a travel agency				

9. Of the following options, which could be applied to this type of trips as a general rule?

❏ I devote the maximum time possible to the observation of wild fauna and/or enjoying the natural landscape on foot, by bicycle, etc. and the rest of the activities are secondary.

❏ The time devoted to nature activities and other types of activities is divided in an equal manner.

❏ The observation of wild fauna and/or contact with unspoiled nature is limited to specific days and occasions.

10. Socio-demographic questions

Age:	❏ 14-29 years of age	❏ 30-39 years of age	❏ 50-59 years of age	❏ 60 and over

Sex:		❏ Male	❏ Female	

• Net monthly income

❏ Less than 250,000 ptas./month	❏ Between 250,000 and 410,000 ptas./month	❏ Over 410,000 ptas./month

• Level of education

❏ Primary	❏ Secondary	❏ University

• Occupation:

• Place of residence

• In which month does your main holiday trip take place:

Thank you for your collaboration

ANNEX 2
Model of survey / interview with specialized operators and agencies

The year 2002 will be "International Year of Ecotourism". As part of the preparatory activities for the event, The World Tourism Organization (WTO) is carrying out a study about the ecotourism market in 5 European countries + USA and Canada, and Planta, S.A. has been commissioned to do it in Spain.

We request that you answer this questionnaire and thank you for your collaboration

The tour operators that collaborate with our work will be named in the study, receive a final edition and receive information about the "International Year of Ecotourism" programme.

PROFILE OF THE COMPANY

COMPANY DETAILS	
• Name:	
• Address:	
• Telephone:	• Fax:
• E-mail:	• WEB:
• Name of the person who is answering this questionnaire:	
• Position:	

WEIGHT AND POSITIONING IN THE SPANISH MARKET	
• Number of employees:	
• Number of branches:	
• Amount of business in the year 2000:	
• Number of products offered:	• N° passengers/year:
• %Sources:	• % Receptive:

KNOWLEDGE OF THE TERMS 'NATURE TOURISM' AND 'ECOTOURISM'

The World Tourism Organization's (WTO) definition of these terms:

- **Nature Tourism:** All types of tourism based on nature, where the main motive is observation and appreciation of nature, as well as traditional cultures.

- **Ecotourism:** Ecotourism is a type of tourism in areas rarely frequented by man, which should contribute to the protection of nature and the welfare of the local populations.

1. It should include the interpretation of nature and pedagogical aspects.

2. Although it is not essential, it is generally organized for small groups by small local companies. Foreign operators, large and small, also organize, set in motion and/or market ecotourism routes, generally for small groups.

3. It minimizes the negative impacts on the natural and the socio-cultural environments.

4. It provides resources for the protection of nature sites:

  - Generating economic benefits for the local communities, the organizations and the authorities that manage these sites with a view to their protection and conservation,

  - Creating jobs and generating (alternative) income for the local communities, making the local populations and the tourists aware of the importance of culture and nature conservation.

1. Do you agree with the WTO's definition of the term 'ecotourism'?

❑ Yes, I agree completely   ❑ Yes, I agree, more or less
❑ Not completely   ❑ No, I disagree completely

2. Do you use the term 'ecotourism' in marketing to promote your company or products?

❑ Yes.   ❑ No

3. Do you think this concept has a future?

❏ Yes   ❏ No

4. Are you in favour of developing this concept among Spanish travel agents?

❏ Yes   ❏ No

5. What are the specific methods for developing this concept and positioning it in the Spanish market?:

❏ Distribute a code of ethical behaviour ("good practices") for travellers/tourists among your clients?

❏ Draw up and adopt a code of ethics ("good practices") among travel agents/operators?

❏ Create an association or grouping of travel agents committed to the environment and ecotourism?

❏ Give your company and internal ecotourism strategy?

❏ Sell ecotourism products?

❏ Organize a national awareness campaign about ecotourism?

❏ Others

THE PRODUCTS

6. Which destinations do you programme for ecotourism products?

	In particular, which countries are preferable:
❏ Africa	_____
❏ Latin America	_____
❏ North America	_____
❏ Caribbean	_____
❏ Asia	_____
❏ Europe:	_____
❏ Middle East	_____
❏ Oceania	_____

7. What themes do you include in the ecotourism products?

- ❑ Exploration trails
- ❑ Sport trekking (walks)
- ❑ Nature trekking
- ❑ Sustainable hunting/fishing
- ❑ Trips with naturalist interest
- ❑ Observation of fauna
- ❑ Protected areas
- ❑ Forests / selviculture
- ❑ Ornithology – bird-watching.
- ❑ Botanical, medicinal plant walks
- ❑ Vulcanology
- ❑ Geology / palaeontology
- ❑ Astronomy
- ❑ Scientific research, study trips.

- ❑ Eco-volunteering. Solidarity tourism related to the environment.
- ❑ Support for and collaboration with conservation programmes.
- ❑ Natural/cultural heritage
- ❑ Traditional products of the region
- ❑ Ethnology / ethnography
- ❑ Cultures of the world
- ❑ Indigenous and traditional communities. Coexistence, stays.
- ❑ Learning local techniques
- ❑ Others, please specify:_____
  _____
  _____

8. Are the following aspects important for you?

(mark from 1 to 4, that is: Unimportant: 1; Not very important: 2; Quite important: 3; Very important: 4)

	1	2	3	4
Respect for the natural environment				
Interpretation of nature				
Trips in small groups				
Integration in the socio-cultural environment (job creation at a local level)				

THE DESTINATIONS

9. What are your clients preferred ecotourism destinations?

- ❑ In Spain
- ❑ In Europe
- ❑ Outside Europe:
  - ❑ Africa
  - ❑ Latin America
  - ❑ North America
  - ❑ Caribbean
  - ❑ Asia
  - ❑ Middle East
  - ❑ Oceania

In particular, most requested areas-countries:

_____
_____
_____
_____
_____
_____
_____
_____
_____

10. How are sales of ecotourism trips distributed among the following destinations:

	% of sales	% of trips
In Spain		
In Europe		
Outside Europe:		

11. Average duration of ecotourism package trips:

	Spain	Europe:	Outside Europe:
Less than one week	❑	❑	❑
1 week	❑	❑	❑
2 weeks	❑	❑	❑
3 weeks	❑	❑	❑
Over 3 weeks	❑	❑	❑

12. Do you think these packages are:

❑ Pure ecotourism products, where the main reason for the trips is ecotourism.

❑ Ecotourism products combined with conventional content at 50%.

❑ Conventional packages with a few days or an excursion with ecotourism content.

THE CLIENTELE

13. Can you describe the typical profile of your ecotourist client for us?

❑ Age:

0 – 19 years old:_____%	20 – 39 years old:_____%
40 – 59 years old_____%	60 – 74 years old:_____%
75 years old and over: _____%	

❑ Males: _____%   ❑ Females: _____%

❑ Socio-economic category:

Higher categories and university professions	_____ %
Medium-level categories and professions:	_____ %
Employees, clerks:	_____ %
Labourers:	_____ %

❑ Net monthly salary:	%
Less than 250,000 ptas./month (1,500 euros)	
Between 250,000 and 400,000 ptas./month (1,500 to 2,400 euros)	
Over 400,000 ptas./month (over 2,400 euros)	

❑ Geographical origin	%
Barcelona metropolitan area	
Barcelona metropolitan area	
Basque Country	
Valencia	
Other areas, please specify	

14. Seasonal variation of the trips:

Summer _____%   Winter _____ %

15. What are your clients' main reasons for going on a nature trip?

❑ Photo safari
❑ Contemplation of outstanding landscapes
❑ Contemplation of wild fauna (large animals)
❑ Encounters and coexistence with indigenous populations
❑ Visits to National Parks
❑ Sporting activities (trekking, rafting)
❑ Others. Please specify

16. Decisive behaviour for classifying a client of a tour operators as an ecotourist

❑ Financial contribution to destination communities.
❑ Participatory products, volunteers
❑ Travel to recognized ecotourism destinations.
❑ Request for highly detailed information
❑ Choice of an operator that keeps to an ethical code of good practice.
❑ Choice of an exploration / nature / cultural product

YOUR CHANNELS OF COMMUNICATION

17. How do you manage to publicize your nature tourism products among those private clients?. What are the most adequate (effective) information - communication media?.

❑ Catalogue / brochure
❑ Personalized promotion / research among target groups and collectives.
❑ Inserts in specialized magazines
❑ Press articles
❑ Specialized trade fairs and shows
❑ Through associations
❑ Through NGOs
❑ Internet
❑ Word of mouth
❑ Loyalty programmes
❑ Others, please specify:

WEIGHT OF NATURE TOURISM AND ECOTOURISM IN YOUR COMPANY

18. Based on the definitions presented above, can you evaluated the weight of these markets in your company?

What percentage of your clientele make reservations?
❑ Nature stays: _____%
❑ Ecotourism stays: _____ %

19. How has your amount of business evolved over the last 3 years with respect to:

What you generally offer	What you offer in the line of ecotourism
❑ Increase	❑ Increase
❑ Stabilization	❑ Stabilization
❑ Reduction	❑ Reduction

20. How do you think the ecotourism segment will evolve in the coming years?

In your sales	The Spanish market
❑ Increase	❑ Increase
❑ Stabilization	❑ Stabilization
❑ Reduction	❑ Reduction

YOUR IMPLICATION IN ECOTOURISM

21. What information does your company make available to clients?

❑ Information dossier prior to the trip
❑ Information files on fauna/flora that are endangered, or threatened with extinction
❑ Information file on conservation programmes
❑ Meetings prior to the start of the trip
❑ Code of good practice or charter of ethical behaviour
❑ Assessment questionnaire to be answered by the client after the trip

22. Do you encourage your clients to make donations to local conservation and development projects?

❑ Yes How? _____
❑ No

Does your company favour the use of local providers/suppliers?

❑ Yes
❑ No

23. Does your company finance or participate in local environmental protection programmes?

❑ Yes. Please specify_____
❑ No

24. Does your company participate or involve itself in collaboration / co-operation action regarding protected areas?

❏ Yes. With what type of stays? How? _____

_____

❏ No

---

25. Is your company an associated member of any organism/organisation for nature protection?

❏ Yes. Please specify _____

_____

❏ No

---

26. Would your company be prepared to invest in favour of your providers/suppliers in any of the following ways?

YES/NO

❏ Advise them on the setting up of their products, permitting them to benefit from your company's experience.

❏ Improve their features and include their products in your company's brochure.

❏ Assume the role of consultant/advisor and privileged partner in order to aid the production and marketing of ecotourism and nature tourism products.

THANK YOU FOR YOUR COLLABORATION

MODEL OF SURVEY/INTERVIEW FOR TOURIST OFFICES

PROFILE OF THE DESTINATION

COMPANY DETAILS	
• Name:	
• Address:	
• Telephone:	• Fax:
• E-mail:	• WEB:
• Name of the person who is answering this questionnaire:	
• Position:	

WEIGHT AND POSITIONING OF THE DESTINATION IN THE SPANISH MARKET
• Number of employees:
• Number of offices:
• Number of passengers:
• % through agencies and operators:
• % of independent trips:

KNOWLEDGE OF THE TERMS 'NATURE TOURISM' AND 'ECOTOURISM'

> **The World Tourism Organization's (WTO) definition of these terms:**
>
> • **Nature Tourism:** All types of tourism based on nature, where the main motive is observation and appreciation of nature, as well as traditional cultures.
>
> • **Ecotourism :** Ecotourism is a type of tourism in areas rarely frequented by humans, which should contribute to the protection of nature and the welfare of the local population.
>
> 1. It should include the interpretation of nature and pedagogical aspects.
>
> 2. Although this is not essential, it is generally organized for small groups by small local companies. Foreign operators, large and small, also organize, set in motion and/or market ecotourism routes, generally for small groups.
>
> 3. It minimizes the negative impact on the natural and the socio-cultural environments.
>
> 4. It provides resources for the protection of nature sites:

• Generating economic benefits for the local communities, the organizations and the authorities that manage these sites with a view to their protection and conservation,

• Creating jobs and generating (alternative) income for the local communities, making the local population and tourists aware of the importance of culture and nature conservation.

1. Do you agree with the WTO's definition of the term 'ecotourism'?

❏ Yes, I agree completely   ❏ Yes, I agree, more or less

❏ Not completely   ❏ No, I disagree completely

2. Do you use the term ecotourism in marketing to promote your destination?

❏ Yes   ❏ No

3. Do you think this concept has a future?

❏ Yes   ❏ No

4. Are you in favour of developing this concept among Spanish travel agents?

❏ Yes   ❏ No

5. What are the specific methods for developing this concept and positioning it in the Spanish market?:

❏ Distribute a code of ethical behaviour ("good practices") for travellers/tourists among your clients?

❏ Draw up and adopt a code of ethics ("good practices") among travel agents/operators?

❏ Create an association or grouping of travel agents committed to the environment and ecotourism?

❏ Give your company and internal ecotourism strategy?

❏ Sell ecotourism products?

❏ Organize a national awareness campaign about ecotourism?

❏ Others

THE PRODUCTS

---

6. What % of trips to your destination does ecotourism represent?

---

7. What themes do you include in the ecotourism products?

❑ Exploration trails
❑ Sport trekking (walks)
❑ Nature trekking
❑ Sustainable hunting/fishing
❑ Trips with naturalist interest
❑ Observation of fauna
❑ Protected areas
❑ Forests / selviculture
❑ Ornithology – bird-watching.
❑ Botanical, medicinal plant walks
❑ Vulcanology
❑ Geology / palaeontology
❑ Astronomy
❑ Scientific research, study trips.   ❑

Eco-volunteering. Solidarity tourism related to the environment.
❑ Support for and collaboration with conservation programmes.
❑ Natural/cultural heritage
❑ Traditional products of the region
❑ Ethnology / ethnography
❑ Cultures of the world
❑ Indigenous and traditional communities. Coexistence, stays.
❑ Learning local techniques
❑ Others, please specify_____
_____
_____

---

8. Have you noticed an increase in what is offered in the line of ecotourism: ❑ Yes   ❑ No

❑ If so, in which subsegments: _____

---

9. Are the following aspects important for you? .
(mark from 1 to 4, that is: Unimportant: 1; Not very important: 2; Quite important: 3; Very important: 4)

	1	2	3	4
Respect for the natural environment				
Interpretation of nature				
Trips in small groups				
Integration in the socio-cultural environment (job creation at local level)				

THE DESTINATIONS

10. What are your country's most popular ecotourism destinations?	

11. What % of tourist traffic and sales correspond to ecotourism destinations in your country.		
	% of traffic	% sales

12. Average duration of ecotourism package trips:
Less than one week
1 week
2 weeks
3 weeks
Over 3 weeks

13. Do you think these packages are:
❑ Pure ecotourism products, where the main reason for the trips is ecotourism.
❑ Ecotourism products combined with conventional content at 50%.
❑ Conventional packages with a few days or an excursion with ecotourism content.

THE CLIENTELE

---

14. Can you describe the typical profile of your ecotourist client for us?

❑ Age:

0 – 19 years old:_____%	20 – 39 years old:_____%
40 – 59 years old_____%	60 – 74 years old:_____%
75 years old and over: _____%	

❑ Males: _____%   ❑ Females: _____%

❑ Socio-economic category:

Higher categories and university professions	_____ %
Medium-level categories and professions:	_____ %
Employees, clerks:	_____ %
Labourers:	_____ %

❑ Net monthly salary:	%
Less than 250,000 ptas./month (1,500 euros)	
Between 250,000 and 400,000 ptas./month (1,500 to 2,400 euros)	
Over 400,000 ptas./month (over 2,400 euros)	

❑ Geographical origin	%
Barcelona metropolitan area	
Barcelona metropolitan area	
Basque Country	
Valencia	
Other areas, please specify	

---

15. Seasonal variation of the trips:

Summer _____%   Winter _____ %

---

16. What are your clients' main reasons for going on a nature trip?

❑ Photo safari

❑ Contemplation of outstanding landscapes

❑ Contemplation of wild fauna (large animals)

❑ Encounters and coexistence with indigenous populations

❑ Visits to National Parks

❑ Sporting activities (trekking, rafting)

❑ Others. Please specify

17. How has ecotourism demand for your destination developed, compared with tourist traffic in general?

› the same › more › less

18. Decisive behaviour for classifying a client of a tour operators as an ecotourist

❑ Financial contribution to destination communities.
❑ Participatory products, volunteers
❑ Travel to recognized ecotourism destinations.
❑ Request for highly detailed information
❑ Choice of an operator that keeps to an ethical code of good practice.
❑ Choice of an exploration / nature / cultural product

YOUR CHANNELS OF COMMUNICATION

19. How do you manage to publicize your nature tourism products among those private clients?. What are the most adequate (effective) information - communication media?.

❑ Catalogue / brochure
❑ Personalized promotion / research among target groups and collectives.
❑ Inserts in trade magazines
❑ Press articles
❑ Specialized trade fairs and shows
❑ Through associations
❑ Through NGOs
❑ Internet
❑ Word of mouth
❑ Loyalty programmes
❑ Others, please specify: _____

WEIGHT OF NATURE TOURISM AND ECOTOURISM IN YOUR DESTINATION

20. Based on the definitions presented above, can you evaluate the weight of these markets in your company?

What percentage of your clientele make reservations?

❑ Nature stays: _____ %
❑ Ecotourism stays: _____ %

21. How do you think the ecotourism segment will evolve in the coming years?

International traffic to your destination	In the Spanish market
❑ Increase	❑ Increase
❑ Stabilization	❑ Stabilization
❑ Reduction	❑ Reduction

YOUR IMPLICATION IN ECOTOURISM

22. What information does your service make available to the clients?

❑ Information dossier prior to the trip

❑ Information files on fauna/flora that are endangered, or threatened with extinction

❑ Information file on conservation programmes

❑ Code of good practice or charter of ethical behaviour

❑ Others. Please specify _____

Thank you for your collaboration

Annex 3:
Tour operators contacted

TOUR OPERATOR	CONTACT	TELEPHONE	ADDRESS	POST CODE	E-MAIL	WEB	PROFILE
ATYPICAL TRAVEL (Barcelona)	Manager: Mr. Victor Muntante	902 118848 F:93 2061015	Gosol, 21	08017-Barcelona	info@atypical-travel.com	www.atypical-travel.com	Adventure, mountaineering, nature
AVIOTEL (Madrid)		91 5561293 F:91 4170365	Capitan Haya, 9 Interior	28020-Madrid	madrid@aviotel.com	www.aviotel.com	Nature
DESTINO	Manager: Ms. Susan Fernández	91 5042020 F:91 5042844	Pez Volador, 32	28007-Madrid	pmtomas@destino.crossinf.com		Nature
ICU VIAJES S.A.* (Central)	Manging Director: Mr. Hernan Arjona	916511015 F:91 6530029	Bilbao, 1 Local 2	28100 (Alcobendas) Madrid	info@icu.es	www.icu.es	Adventure and nature trekking
KUONI (Central)	Manging Director: Mr. Daniel Ponzo Directora T.O.: Ms. Sonsoles Alvare	91 5382700 F:91 5382727	Pº Infanta Maria Isabel, 17, 1º	28014-Madrid	kuoni@kuoni.es	www.kuoni.es	Nature Filial in Spain of KUONI Switzerland
BAOBAB TOURS V.		93 2800343 F: 93 2804508	Gran Capitan s/n	08034-Barcelona	info@baobab.es	www.baobab.es	Retailer. Adventure Nature
NUBA	Product Manager	91 7454747	Maria de Molina, 46	28006-Madrid	correo@nuba.net		Retailer.
EXPEDICIONES V	Elisa Alday	F: 91 5620490					Expeditions. Adventure
UCPA* Skipass (Delegación Madrid)		91 4426060 F:91 4424464	Rios Rosas, 7	28003-Madrid	javiersanchez@ skypass.crossinf.com	www.ucpa.fr	Retailer. Expeditions. Adventure
ASECOTUR (Central)	Manager: Mr. Francisco García Luque/ Rosa Plaza	91 6740513/ 91 6740711 F:91 6740414	Los Llanos de Jerez, 5	28820-Coslada (Madrid)	vasecotu@idecnet.com rosa@asecomex.com		Nature, trekking
DIMENSIONES (Central)*	Mr. Emiliano Hernández Managing Director: Mr.Felix Estevez	91 5310607/ 91 5314162 F:91 5214254	Jacometerzo, 4, pl.11 (atico)	28013-Madrid	dimensiones@intelred.es	www.viajesdimensiones.es	Adventure and nature. Routes
DE VIAJE V.	Augusto	91 5779899 F: 91775756	Serrano, 41	28001-Madrid	agencia@deviaje.com	www.deviaje.com	Retailer
VIAJES ALTAIR (ORIXÁ Viajes)	César García	91 5435300 F: 91 544 34 98	Gaztambide. 31	28015-Madrid	madrid@orixa.com	www.orixa.com	Specialized library
EXPOMUNDO / ULTRAMAR Express		91 3198175 F:91 3086502	Zurbano, 56	28010-Madrid	uexzurbano@uex.es		Nature

TOUR OPERATOR	CONTACT	TELEPHONE	ADDRESS	POST CODE	E-MAIL	WEB	PROFILE
DIMENSIONES (Delegation)		93 3131365 F: 93 3137466	Concilio de Trento, 182-184	08020-Barcelona	icanto@viajes dimensiones.com	www.viajes dimensiones.com	Nature
INTERMUNDOS (Central)	Adela y Jose Mª. (decision-markers for Central America) Sales Manager: Mr. Miguel Angel Giménez	91 5320413 F:91 5221241	Fuencarral, 9, 1º	28004-Madrid	comerci@intermun.com	www.intermundos.com	Nature
NOUVELLES FRONTIERES	Manager: Mr. Joan Boada. Sales Manager: Michelle	93 4857907 / 902170979 F:933027158 / 902 11 97 62	Balmes, 8, Bajos	08007-Barcelona	m.purrieu@nouvelles-frontieres.es	www.nouvelles-frontieres.es	Adventure and nature trekking. Wholesaler of the Nouvelles Frontiers group
NUESTROS CAMINOS	Manager: Mr. Ballesteros	91 5475300/ 91 547 2509 F:91 5471792	Gran Via, 66, 6º, 17	28013-Madrid	(aun no tienen e-mail)	www.nuestroscaminos.es	Nature. Cultural
PREMIER TOURS	Managing Director: Mr. Jose Luis Leza	93 2151282/ 93 2151350 F:93 2151172	Mallorca, 277, 2º	08037-Barcelona	premier@accesocero.es	www.premier-tours.com	Nature
TIERRA JOVEN (Central)	Manager: Mr. Juan Ranchal	91 5317708 F:91 5231620/28	San Bernardo, 20, 3º	28015-Madrid	tjinformacion@ tierrajoven.com	www.tierrajoven.com	Adventure and nature
TIERRAS INEDITAS Viajes Bidon5	Manager: Ms. Carmen Arrieta	91 5476117/ 91 5480490 F:91 5423848	Juan de Dios, 5, 1ª Izda.	28015-Madrid	tierras@incomix.es	www.encomix.es/ tierras/ineditas	Adventure, mountaineering nature, trekking
TRAPSATUR*	Managing Director: Mr. Antonio Pedraz	91 5426666 F:91 5420719	San Bernardo, 5 y 7	28013-Madrid	trapsatur@attglobal.net	www.eol.es/trapsatur	Nature
U.C.P.A.-SKIPASS/ MAR (Central)		93 2251875	Pº Juan de Borgoña, 92, 4º	08003-Barcelona		www.ucpa.fr	Nature, trekking
AkALI	Manager: Mr. Jose Luis Barragán	91 4484158 F:91 4484258	Menendez Vadés, 17	28015-Madrid	vgram@bcsnetwork.es vgram@grupoeuropa.com	www.viajesgram.com	Adventure

TOUR OPERATOR	CONTACT	TELEPHONE	ADDRESS	POST CODE	E-MAIL	WEB	PROFILE
AÑOS LUZ (Central)	Manging Director: Mr. Mariano Sanz Vaquero /Iñigo Krug	94 4 24 22 15 F:94 4235593	Berasategui, 4, Bajo Izda.	48001-Bilbao	aluz_bio@jet.es	www.aluz.com	Adventure, nature, trekking. Retailer. Alternative tourism
EXPLORER. VIAJEROS.	Managing Director: Mr. Francisco Javier Benavides	93 4522525 F: 93 4543215	Pl. Dr. Letamendi, 37, 5°, 3ª	08007-Barcelona	viajeros@redestb.es		Adventure, nature,, mountaineering rural tourism
LEXITOURS	Manager: Mr.Juan José Redondo	91 5220203 F: 91 5221395	C/. Del Carmen, 17, 2°	28013-Madrid	lexi@lexitours.org	www.lexitours.org	Adventure, trekking, mountaineering
NORDIKUM	Manager: Mr. Juan Ramón Formatjet	93 4514186 F:93 4514807	Provenza, 220	08036-Barcelona	nordikum@nordikum.com	www.nordikum.com	Adventure, nature
NUEVAS RUTAS SKI & AVENTURA (Madrid Delegation)		91 4179983 F:91 5556962	P° Castellana, 77, Edif. Cristalería, 3°	28046-Madrid			Adventure. Also rural and ecotourism
CATAI TOURS (Central)	Head of Ecotourism Product: Fernando Sánchez Dorctor. Manager: Ms. Matilde Torres	91 4091125/ 914093281 F:914096692/ 91 5044207	O'Donnell, 49	28009-Madrid	catai@catai.es	www.catai.es	Adventure, trekking
CLASS TOUR-EVATOUR	Director General: Sr. Antonio Vicario	91 597 09 26 F:91 5970059	Av. del Brasil, 4,2ª, of. 2	28020-Madrid	booking@evatours-classtour.es	www.evatours-classtour.com	Adventure, trekking
TIEMPO LIBRE. MUNDICOLOR (Central)	Managing Director: Mr. Julio González Soria	91 4568600 F:91 456 8773/ 74/75/76	Sor Angela de la Cruz, 6, 10°	28020-Madrid	mundicolor@mundicolor.es emisor@mundicolor.es	www.mundicolor.es	Adventure
ATYPICAL TRAVEL (Madrid)		902 118848 F: 91 5484159	Gran Via, 88,G 4, Piso 15, Of. 12	28013-Madrid	info@atypical-travel.com	www.atypical-travel.com	Adventure
AVIOTEL (Barcelona)	Manager: Mr. Daniel Tejedor. Sales Manager: Mr. Ramón Martínez	93 3011213- 93 3011784 F:93 3184674	Gran Via Corts Catalanes, 645, 7°, 12ª	08010-Barcelona	comercial@aviotel.com	www.aviotel.com	Nature
TURISGROUP (Central)	Manager: Mr. Manuel Cerradedo	93 4153845 F: 93 2173691	Av. Princeps Dásturies, 37	08012-Barcelona	tgroup@cconline.es		Adventure

TOUR OPERATOR	CONTACT	TELEPHONE	ADDRESS	POST CODE	E-MAIL	WEB	PROFILE
MATX	Manager: Ms. Mª Dolores Roca Cortes	973 451198 F: 973 451434	Pº Estación, 11	25600-Balaguer (Lerida)	matx.x@iltrida.com	www.iltrida.com	Nature
SIGUENOS	Manager: Mr. Enrique Torres	96 3916869 F: 96 3911739	Gran Via Fernando el Católico, 24	46008-Valencia	siguenos@ctv.es		Nature
CLUB MARCO POLO	Jose Luis Angulo.	91 364.11.46 F:91 364.13.93	Plaza Mayor, 1, 1ª	28012-Madrid	mad@clubmarcopolo.es	www.clubmarcopolo.es/	Travellers club alternative trips
ITSASLUR	Coli Fernández / Amaya Irigoyen	948 150361- 242791/ 908 778890 F: 948 150275	Goroabe, 25	31.005-Pamplona	itsaslur@grupogea.com		Retailer. Alternative tourism, trekking, "unconventional" destinations
BANOA	Xavier Roman	93 318.96.00 F:93 318.00.37	Ronda de Sant Pere, 11 - Atico 3º	08010-Barcelona	bcn@banoa.com		Specialized retailer. Alternative and ecological. Tourism trekking
TREKKING Y. AVENTURA V	Jose Antonio	91 5228681 F: 5231664	Del Pez,12	28004-Madrid	mad@trekki ngviajes.com	www.trekkingviajes.com/	Retailer. Trekking. Unconventional countries. (Little ecotourism)
TUAREG V. (P)	Franchesca Marsá.	93 210.55.11/ 265.23.91 F:93 2848747- 2651070	Consell de Cent 378	08009-Barcelona	tuareg@cambrabcn.es	www.tuaregviatges.es	Retailer. Alternative trips. "Strange" destinations. (In theory, no ecotourism)
BIDON 5 V.	Anabel (does not work there) ATT ANA	91 5476117 F:91 5423848	Juan de Dios, 5, 1º izda.	28015-Madrid	travel@bidon5.es	www.bidon5.es	Retailer. Alternative tourism, trekking, etc.
AVIAL-ASTROLABIO	Mr. Jesús Zamarriego	91 447.80.00 F:91 447.98.09	Santisima . Trinidad, 15	28010-Madrid	avial@grupoeuropa.com		Retailer. Alternative trips. Active tourism. Exotic countries
AÑOS LUZ (Delegation)	José Larrea	91 4451145- 44559621 F:91 593918	San Bernardo, 97-99	28015-Madrid	aluz_mad@jet.es	www.aluz.com	Retailer. Alternative trips. Active tourism. Exotic countries

TOUR OPERATOR	CONTACT	TELEPHONE	ADDRESS	POST CODE	E-MAIL	WEB	PROFILE
N.E.W.S ACTIVIDADES	Ms. Dominique Morata Mr. Bruno Anguita	91 5314028 F: 91 5315565	Mayor, 6, 6º izda.	28013-Madrid	newsviajes@gmx.net	(Under construction)	Retailer. Ecological and adventure tourism
AMBAR- OTROS VIAJES	Antonio Cordero	91 3645912 F: 91 3540085	Cava Alta, 17	28005-Madrid	info@ambarviajes.com		Specialized retailer. Trips with character
NOBEL (Central)	Sales Manager: Carlos González. Manager: Mr.Antonio Pelegrín	91 372 79 00 F:917080225	Gobelas, 21, 1º Dcha.	28023-Madrid	promo@nobeltur.com	www.nobel-tour.com www.indoriente.com	Adventure
VIAJES EL CORTE INGLES (Central)	Head of Department: Beatriz López de Quesada	91 3298100 F:91 7470174	Av. de Cantabria, 51	28042-Madrid		viajes.elcorteingles.es	Important tour operator. Important sales network of 100 retail agencies
UNIJOVEN (Central)	Ms. Maribel Redondo Managing Director Mr. José Miguel Aparicio Manager: Jeús Pérez	91 5219000 F:91 5596102 3, of. 3, puerta 3	Gran Via, 88, Ed. España, Grupo	28013- Madrid	info@unijoven.es	ww.unijoven.es	Routes for young people All over the world. Ecotourism programme; "Tourism and nature"
TRANSRUTAS (Madrid Delegation)	Victor Ranedo	91 5798200 F:91 5798191	Rosario Pino, 6, 9º B	28013-Madrid.	reservasmad@ transrutas.redesteb.es	www.transrutas.com	Routes
JUVENTUS TRAVEL, S.A.	Jesús Caballero (Sales Manager)	91 3194149 F: 91 3194813	Fernando VI, 9	28004-Madrid	juventustravel@yahoo.es		Travel Agency.
ACTUR - VALLE ARAN	Manager: José Manuel Villanova	91 531 01 71 / 532 9646	Espoz y Mina, 3, 1º dcha.	28001- Madrid	administracion@actur.com		Rural Tourism. Adventure
CULTURA AFRICANA	Manager: Javier Lago	91 539 32 67	S. Eugenio. 8 1 dcha.	28001- Madrid	cafrica@oem.es		
VALUE	Germán o juan Goyare	91 401 59 59/ 402 04 55 F: 91 402 04 55	Diego de León 69		value@retemail.es		
MARFIL Viajes	Koldo	948 29 03 50		Navarra	koldo@marfilviajes.com		
MUZTAG - Cota 8000	Enrique Ripoll	93 2850261		Barcelona	muztag@retemail.es		

ANNEX 4
Analysis of brochures / catalogues

8 brochures / catalogues are examined below.

1. AÑOS LUZ

All 79 pages of the brochure are devoted to tourism with a natural air, devoting 50% to ecotourism products combined with conventional ones, and the rest divided between pure ecotourism and conventional products with the odd excursion with ecotourism content.

They offer 90 destinations in:

	Especially in:
• Africa	Tanzania
• Latin America	Peru
• North America	USA and Canada
• Caribbean	Cuba
• Asia	Myanmar (Burma)
	Vietnam
• EUROPE:	The Alps
• Middle East	Egypt
• Oceania	Australia

Being, in the most part, from Asia and America.

The offer in Spain is minimal, offering nature trips to:

- Asturias
- Cádiz (Sierra de Grazalema)
- Pyrenees
- Canary Islands
- Balearic Islands

They include 122 products:

• Exploration trails • Sport trekking (walks) • Nature trekking • Trips with naturalist interest • Observation of fauna • Protected areas • Forests / selviculture • Ornithology – bird-watching. • Botanical, medicinal plant walks • Vulcanology • Geology / palaeontology	• Astronomy (tailor-made) • Scientific research, study trips.(tailor-made projects) • Eco-volunteering. Solidarity tourism related to the environment. • Support for and collaboration with conservation programmes. • Natural/cultural heritage • Traditional products of the region • Ethnology / ethnography • Cultures of the world • Indigenous and traditional communities. Coexistence, stays.

The average price is 250,000/300,000 ptas. (1,500/1,800 euros)/21 days, including flight, accommodation, transfers and insurance.

2. MARCO POLO

45-page brochure. All its packages combine ecotourism and conventional content, at 50%.

They offer 41 destinations, none of them in Spain. The preferred destinations of ecotourism clients are:

	Especially in:
• Caribbean •Asia	Costa Rica Vietnam India Myanmar (Burma)

They include:

• Exploration trails • Sport trekking (walks) • Observation of fauna	• Astronomy (tailor-made) • Natural/cultural heritage • Indigenous and traditional communities. Coexistence, stays.

The average price is 250,000/300,000 ptas.(1,500/1,800 euros)/21 days, including flight, accommodation, transfers and insurance.

3. ORIXA

44-page brochure.

They offer 20 destinations in:

	Especially in:
• Africa	India
• Latin America	Nepal
• North America	Myanmar (Burma)
• Caribbean	Vietnam
• Asia	Laos
• Europe:	Cambodia
• Middle East	Yemen
• Oceania	Iran

They include:

• Exploration trails	• Vulcanology
• Nature trekking	• Geology / palaeontology
• Trips with naturalist interest	• Astronomy (tailor-made)
• Observation of fauna	• Ethnology / ethnography
• Protected areas	• Cultures of the world
• Forests / selviculture	• Indigenous and traditional
• Ornithology – bird-watching.	communities. Coexistence, stays.

The average price, outside Europe, is 250,000/300,000 ptas. (1,500/1,800 euros)/21 days, including flight, accommodation and transfers.

4. TREKKING AND ADVENTURE

29-page brochure, completely devoted to ecotourism and adventure tourism.

They offer 56 destinations in:

	Especially in:
• Africa	
• Latin America	
• North America	Alaska
• Caribbean	Caribbean
• Asia	
• Europe:	Ireland
• Middle East	

They include 80 products:

• Exploration trails • Sport trekking (walks) • Nature trekking • Trips with naturalist interest • Observation of fauna • Protected areas • Astronomy	• Natural/cultural heritage • Ethnology / ethnography • Cultures of the world • Indigenous and traditional communities. Coexistence, stays. • Sport Trekking, sea-kayaking (Greenland)…

The average price, outside Europe, is 250,000/300,000 ptas./21 days, including flight, accommodation and transfers.

In Spain, they offer only 3 products in the Canary Islands:

• Trekking in Tenerife and La Palma
• Trekking in Lanzarote and Fuerteventura
• Naturalist cruise Tenerife-Gomera-Hierro

Average price: 144,000 ptas.(865 euros)/15 days

5. NUBA

42-page brochure, 50% devoted to ecotourism and ecotourist products with conventional trips.

They offer 34 destinations in:

• Africa
• Latin America
• North America
• Caribbean
• Asia
• Europe
• Middle East
• Oceania

They include 72 products:

• Exploration trails • Sport trekking (walks) • Nature trekking • Trips with naturalist interest • Observation of fauna • Protected areas • Forests / selviculture • Ornithology – bird-watching. • Botanical, medicinal plant walks • Vulcanology • Geology / palaeontology • Astronomy	• Scientific research, study trips. • Eco-volunteering. Solidarity tourism related to the environment. • Support for and collaboration with conservation programmes. • Natural/cultural heritage • Traditional products of the region • Ethnology / ethnography • Cultures of the world • Indigenous and traditional communities. Coexistence, stays. • Learning local techniques

The average price, outside Europe, is 300,000/400,000 ptas.(1,800/2,400 euros)/21 days, including flight, accommodation, transfers and admission to the parks.

In Europe they only programme the Azores, Greenland and Lapland.

6. CULTURA AFRICANA

35-page brochure, 50% devoted to ecotourism and ecotourist products combined with conventional trips.

They offer 28 destinations exclusively in Africa, mainly in:

• Tanzania
• Cameroon
• Mali
• Togo
• Benin
• Uganda
• Ethiopia
• Niger

They include 44 products:

• Nature trekking • Observation of fauna • Natural/cultural heritage • Traditional products of the region • Ethnology / ethnography	• Cultures of the world • Indigenous and traditional communities. Coexistence, stays. • Learning local techniques

The duration of the majority of trips is between 8 and 15 days.

The average price is 250,000/300,000 ptas. 1,500 ptas.(1,800 euros)/15 days

7. AMBAR OTROS VIAJES

Original 100-page brochure, called Pasaporte a la Aventura (Passport to Adventure), which includes photographs, competition details and notes for the trip. All their products are ecotourism.

They offer 44 destinations in:

• Africa
• Latin America
• North America
• Caribbean
• Asia
• Middle East
• Oceania

They include 60 products:

• Exploration trails • Sport trekking (walks) • Nature trekking • Trips with naturalist interest • Observation of fauna • Protected areas • Forests / selviculture • Ornithology – bird-watching.	• Support for and collaboration with conservation programmes. • Natural/cultural heritage • Traditional products of the region • Ethnology / ethnography • Cultures of the world • Indigenous and traditional communities. Coexistence, stays. • Solidarity tourism / responsible tourism

The average price is 250,000/400,000 ptas.(1,500/2,400 euros)/21 days, including flights, accommodation, transfers, guide and companion and full board on the camps.

In Europe they offer only Greenland, as well as a programme called "A todo Trapo – Veleros" (Under full sail - Sailboats) which offers sailboat trips around Holland, Balearic Islands, Greek Islands, Turkey, ...

8. ACTUR VIAJES

Tour operator of mainly rural tourism. They have individual brochures for each destination, with the exception of the one devoted to "Los Grandes Viajes" (Great Voyages). Its products are ecotourism combined with conventional trips at 50%.

"Los Grandes Viajes" (Great Voyages) 6-page brochure, devoted to Iran, Libya and Morocco.

The main destinations are in:

	In particular, what countries are preferable:
• Africa	Maghreb countries
• Asia	Iran, Turkmenistan Pakistan
• Europe	Spain and Portugal
• Middle East	Jordan
• Oceania	

They include 25 products:

• Exploration trails (incentives): • (A lot of) Sport trekking (walks) • Nature trekking • Trips with naturalist interest • Observation of fauna • Protected areas • Vulcanology (tailor-made) • Geology / palaeontology	• Natural/cultural heritage • Traditional products of the region • Ethnology / ethnography • Cultures of the world • Indigenous and traditional communities. Coexistence, stays. • Learning local techniques

Annex 5:
PICTE Survey:
Spanish tourists' stays

Table 1: duration of the stays

	2nd. RESIDENCE		DURATION OF THE TRIP						
	TOTAL	Corta duración	Total	1 a 3	4 a 7	8 a 15	16 a 21	Más de 21	Ns/Nc
TOTAL	123,400,700	77,256,720	46,143,980	16,727,800	14,510,490	9,014,457	1,741,417	3,963,956	185,859
Absolute data									
Abroad	4,100,138	131,248	3,968,890	863,750	1,517,725	1,098,413	161,608	318,671	8,722
Spain	119,144,300	76,969,250	42,175,090	15,864,050	12,992,770	7,916,044	1,579,808	3,645,286	177,137
Horizontal percentages									
TOTAL	123,400,700	62.6	37.4	36.3	31.4	19.5	3.8	8.6	0.4
Abroad	4,100,138	3.2	96.8	21.8	38.2	27.7	4.1	8.0	0.2
Spain	119,144,300	64.6	35.4	37.6	30.8	18.8	3.7	8.6	0.4
Andalusia	17,716,350	54.7	45.3	40.0	28.8	18.8	3.9	8.3	0.2
Aragón	4,085,568	54.7	45.3	44.8	30.9	14.3	3.2	6.6	0.1
Asturias (Principality of)	3,370,898	59.4	40.6	39.6	33.5	19.9	2.7	4.2	–
Balearic Islands	1,980,619	53.6	46.4	15.5	34.4	35.2	2.9	11.8	0.1
Canary Islands	4,758,984	61.4	38.6	34.5	39.6	18.3	1.9	5.4	0.3
Cantabria	3,144,504	64.6	35.4	34.5	33.9	15.8	3.9	11.5	0.5
Castilla-La Mancha	10,237,440	76.0	24.0	42.5	36.0	12.2	3.0	6.1	0.2
Castilla y León	14,300,790	72.5	27.5	44.3	26.8	16.0	3.7	9.0	0.3
Catalonia	18,621,480	71.7	28.3	39.5	29.5	18.9	3.8	7.8	0.5
Comunidad Valenciana	15,716,110	62.7	37.3	25.5	30.1	25.3	5.4	13.4	0.3
Extremadura	3,093,395	52.7	46.3	33.6	32.8	21.4	3.1	8.5	0.7
Galicia	6,516,513	62.9	37.1	27.2	36.7	22.2	4.2	9.5	0.2
Madrid (Comunidad de)	6,860,619	61.3	38.7	66.8	26.7	7.9	2.3	4.3	1.9
Murcia (Región de Murcia)	2,759,592	56.6	43.4	26.6	29.0	24.5	5.4	13.8	0.7
Navarre (Comunidad foral de)	1,912,079	74.3	25.7	45.2	32.6	13.5	4.0	4.5	0.2
Basque country	2,620,183	65.0	35.0	43.1	27.3	18.0	2.6	7.8	1.2
Rioja (La)	1,399,494	72.1	27.9	44.4	35.4	9.3	4.5	5.6	0.8
Ceuta and Melilla	49,722	17.1	82.9	6.5	18.8	48.6	–	26.1	–

Table 2: Breakdown of motives

	TOTAL	Destination Spain	Destination Spain whith hotel accommodation	Foreing destination
TOTAL	**9.1**	**9.1**	**5.4**	**9.7**
MAIN REASON FOR THE JOURNEY				
Work/Business	6.0	5.7	3.7	7.7
Studies	9.0	7.1	5.6	32.3
Visiting family/friends	6.0	5.6	3.1	14.5
Voluntary medical treatment	11.1	11.2	10.2	5.0
Religious reasons	6.7	6.9	3.2	6.0
Leisure/relaxation/holidays	10.4	10.6	5.9	8.5
Others	6.2	5.8	3.4	9.1
Don't know/Don't remember	17.4	18.3	4.3	7.1

Annex 6: Breakdown of question 4 of the tourist survey:

Have you been on an ecotourism trip in the past? (Diagram 4 and 29 in the report)

4.1. Visits to National parks/protected areas in:

SPAIN

	TOTAL	% (s/128)
Andalusia	35	27.34
Aragón	17	13.28
Asturias	21	16.41
Balearic Islands	7	5.47
Canary Islands	10	7.81
Cantabria	13	10.16
Castilla y León	4	3.13
Catalonia	8	6.25
Castilla-La Mancha	11	8.59
Madrid	2	1.56
Total	**128**	100
SPAIN	29	
SPAIN TOTAL	**157**	

Main parks:

	TOTAL	% (s/118)
Cabañeros National Park	3	2.73
Doñana National Park	26	23.64
Órdesa National Park	17	15.45
Picos de Europa National Park	16	14.55
Tablas de Damiel National Park	8	7.27
Aigües Tortes Nature Reserve	3	2.73
Cañadas del Teide Nature Reserve	7	6.36
Garajonay Nature Reserve	5	4.55
Monfragüe Nature Reserve	3	2.73
Somiedo Nature Reserve	2	1.82
Alto Tajo Nature Reserve	2	1.82
Timanfaya National Park	6	5.45
Gredos Nature Reserve	2	1.82
Sierra de Cazorla	8	7.27
Sierra Nevada	2	1.82
Total responses	**110**	100

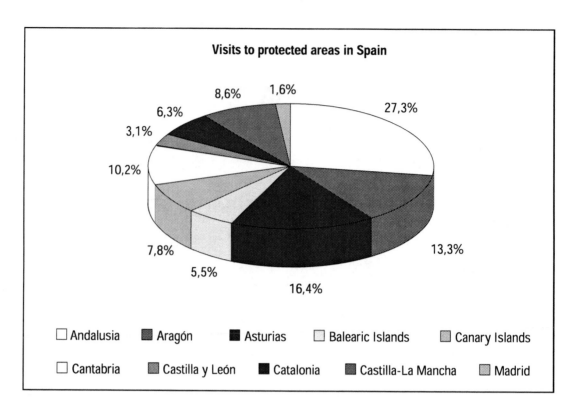

VISITS TO NATIONAL PARKS/PROTECTED AREAS (ALL DESTINATIONS):

AFRICA	TOTAL	% (s/216)
Egypt	2	0,93
Kenya	3	1,39
Mali	2	0,93
Morocco	1	0,46
South Africa	4	1,85
Tunisia	1	0,46
AFRICA TOTAL	13	6,02

EUROPE		
Germany	3	1,39
Austria	2	0,93
Scotland	3	1,39
Spain	109	50,46
France	3	1,39
England	1	0,46
Iceland	1	0,46
Norway	4	1,85
Portugal	3	1,39
Switzerland (The Alps)	3	1,39
EUROPE TOTAL	132	61,11

VISITS TO NATIONAL PARKS/PROTECTED AREAS (ALL DESTINATIONS) (Cont.):

AMERICA	TOTAL	% (s/216)
Argentina	3	1,39
Brazil	12	5,56
Canada	3	1,39
Central America	5	2,31
Colombia	6	2,78
Cuba	5	2,31
USA	9	4,17
Mexico	7	3,24
Peru	4	1,85
Dominican Republic	3	1,39
Venezuela	5	2,31
AMERICA TOTAL	62	28,70
ASIA		
India	4	1,85
Nepal	2	0,93
Thailand	3	1,39
ASIA TOTAL	9	4,17
TOTAL RESPONSES	**216**	**100**

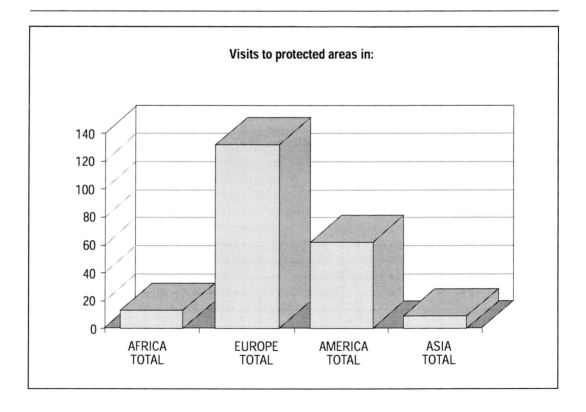

Visits to protected areas in:

4.2. Fauna- and bird-watching in:

ALL DESTINATIONS:

EUROPE	TOTAL	% (s/55)
Germany	3	5,45
Spain	21	38,18
France	1	1,82
Norway	1	1,82
United Kingdom	2	3,64
EUROPE TOTAL	28	50,91
AFRICA	3	
AFRICA TOTAL	3	5,45
AMERICA		
Argentina	3	5,45
Brazil	2	3,64
Caribbean	2	3,64
Costa Rica	1	1,82
Chile	1	1,82
USA	1	1,82
Paraguay	1	1,82
Peru	1	1,82
Venezuela	2	3,64
AMERICA TOTAL	14	25,45
ASIA		
Sri Lanka	2	3,64
India	3	5,45
Nepal	2	3,64
ASIA TOTAL	7	12,73
OCEANIA		
Australia	3	5,45
OCEANIA TOTAL	3	5,45
TOTAL RESPONSES	55	100

SPAIN	TOTAL	% (s/21)
Asturias	1	4,76
Ávila	1	4,76
Cabañeros	1	4,76
Cazorla	2	9,52
Covadonga	1	4,76
Doñana	7	33,33
Spain in general	4	19,05
Extremadura	1	4,76
Monfragüe	1	4,76
The North of Spain	2	9,52
Total Spain	**21**	**100**

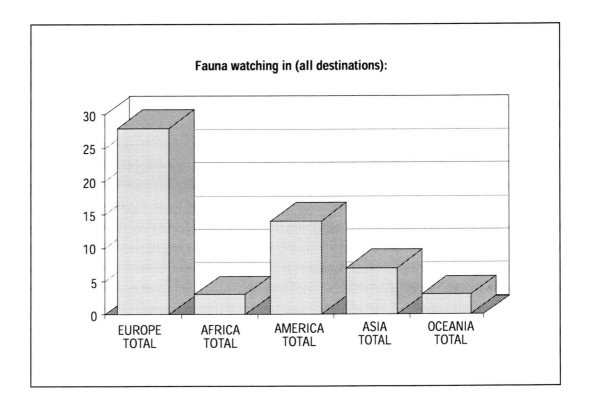

4.3. Trekking

AFRICA	TOTAL	% (s/61)
Morocco (Atlas)	5	8,20
AFRICA TOTAL	5	8,20

AMERICA		
Argentina (Patagonia)	2	3,28
Caribbean	1	1,64
USA (Yellowstone, Yosemite)	3	4,92
Guatemala	1	1,64
Peru (Machu Pichu)	6	9,84
AMERICA TOTAL	13	21,31

ASIA		
Bali	1	1,64
Nepal	2	3,28
Tibet	1	1,64
ASIA TOTAL	4	6,56

EUROPE		
Germany	1	1,64
The Alps	7	11,48
Crete	1	1,64
Spain	23	37,70
France	2	3,28
Iceland	1	1,64
Lapland (Finland)	1	1,64
United Kingdom	2	3,28
Switzerland	1	1,64
EUROPE TOTAL	39	63,93

TOTAL RESPONSES	61	100

ESPAÑA	TOTAL	% (s/23)
Asturias	2	8,70
Camino de Santiago	2	8,70
Navarre	1	4,35
Ordesa National Park	2	8,70
Picos de Europa	4	17,39
The Pyrenees	4	17,39
Requena (Val.)	1	4,35
Sierra de Madrid	4	17,39
Sierra de Gredos	2	8,70
Sierra de Guadarrama	1	4,35
TOTAL SPAIN	**23**	**100**

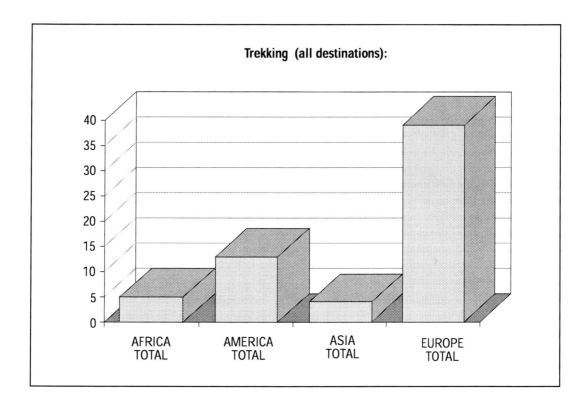

4.4. Exploration trails in:

EUROPE	TOTAL	% (s/26)
Spain	5	19,23
Norway	1	3,85
Sweden	1	3,85
Switzerland	1	3,85
Turkey	1	3,85
EUROPE TOTAL	9	34,62
AFRICA		
Egypt	2	7,69
AFRICA TOTAL	2	7,69
ASIA		
Bali	1	3,85
India	2	7,69
Nepal	2	7,69
ASIA TOTAL	5	19,23
AMERICA		
Brazil (the Amazon)	3	11,54
Colombia	1	3,85
USA	2	7,69
Mexico	1	3,85
Orinoco	1	3,85
Peru	1	3,85
Venezuela	1	3,85
AMERICA TOTAL	10	38,46
TOTAL RESPONSES	**26**	**100**

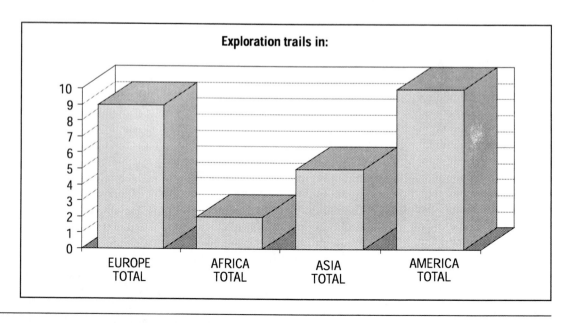

4.5. Nature Sports in:

EUROPE	TOTAL	% (s/39)
Germany	1	2,56
Spain	10	25,64
France	1	2,56
Iceland	1	2,56
Portugal	1	2,56
Switzerland (the Alps)	2	5,13
EUROPE TOTAL	16	41,03
AMERICA		
Belize	1	2,56
Caribbean	3	7,69
Colombia	1	2,56
USA	2	5,13
Mexico	3	7,69
Peru	1	2,56
Venezuela	1	2,56
AMERICA TOTAL	12	30,77
ASIA		
Bali	1	2,56
Malaysia	2	5,13
China Sea	1	2,56
Red Sea	2	5,13
ASIA TOTAL	6	15,38
AFRICA AND OCEANIA		
Australia	4	10,26
Morocco	1	2,56
AFRICA/OCEANIA TOTAL	5	12,82
TOTAL RESPONSES	**39**	**100**

TYPES OF SPORT:

	TOTAL	% (s/33)
Mountain climbing	3	9,1
Diving	7	21,2
Cycling	6	18,2
Water sports (Canoeing	3	9,1
Rafting) Canyoning	3	9,1
Horse-riding	3	9,1
Skiing	3	9,1
Motorcycling	1	3,0
Swimming	1	3,0
Trekking	1	3,0
Surfing	2	6,1
SPORTS TOTAL	**33**	**100,0**

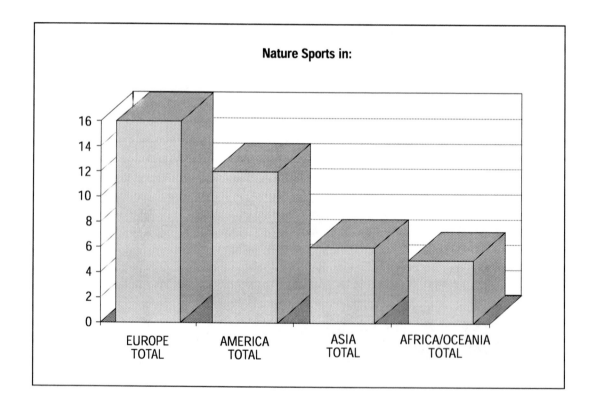

Nature Sports in:

4.6. Naturalist and health trips in:

ESPAÑA	TOTAL	% (s/8)
Alicante	1	12,50
Almería	1	12,50
Asturias	1	12,50
Canary Islands	2	25
Galicia	1	12,50
Madrid	1	12,50
Valle del Teide	1	12,50
SPAIN TOTAL	**8**	**100**

ALL DESTINATIONS:

EUROPE	TOTAL	% (s/18)
Denmark	1	5,56
Spain	8	44,44
France	1	5,56
Iceland	2	11,11
Portugal	1	5,56
EUROPE TOTAL	13	72,22

AMERICA		
the Amazon	2	11,11
Central America	1	5,56
Mexico	1	5,56
Orinoco	1	5,56
Venezuela	1	5,56
AMERICA TOTAL	6	33,33

TOTAL RESPONSES	**19**	**105,56**

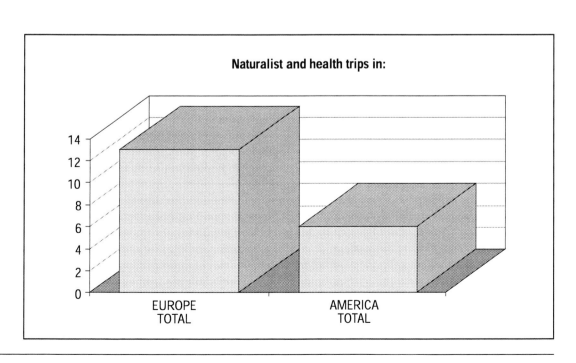

Naturalist and health trips in:

4.7. Adventure, multi-adventure in:

SPAIN	TOTAL	% (s/11)
Aragón	2	18,18
Cabañeros	1	9,09
Castilla y León	2	18,18
Cuenca	1	9,09
the North	2	18,18
Basque Country	1	9,09
The Pyrenees	2	18,18
TOTAL RESPONSES	**11**	**100**

ALL DESTINATIONS:		
ÁFRICA	**TOTAL**	**%**
Burkina Faso	1	3,85
Ivory Coast	1	3,85
Guinea	1	3,85
Mali	2	7,69
the Nile	1	3,85
AFRICA TOTAL	6	23,08
AMERICA		
Brazil	2	7,69
Cuba	1	3,85
Uruguay	1	3,85
AMERICA TOTAL	4	15,38
ASIA		
India	1	3,85
the Orient	1	3,85
ASIA TOTAL	2	7,69
EUROPE		
Spain	11	42,31
Finland	1	3,85
Portugal	1	3,85
Romania	1	3,85
EUROPE TOTAL	14	53,85
TOTAL RESPONSES	**26**	**100**

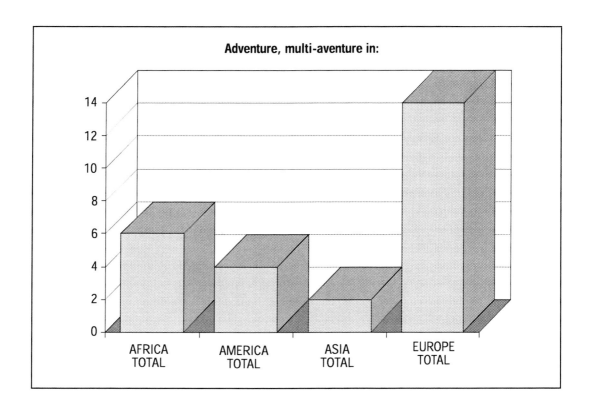

4.8.Cultural trips in :

ÁFRICA	TOTAL	% (s/78)
Algeria	1	1,28
Burkina Faso	1	1,28
Ivory Coast	1	1,28
Egypt	7	8,97
Mali	1	1,28
Morocco	4	5,13
South Africa	1	1,28
Tunisia	1	1,28
AFRICA TOTAL	17	21,79

AMERICA		
Argentina	1	1,28
Bolivia	1	1,28
Brazil	3	3,85
Central America	1	1,28
Colombia	1	1,28
Cuba	1	1,28
Mexico	2	2,56
Peru	1	1,28
Dominican Republic	1	1,28
Venezuela	1	1,28
AMERICA TOTAL	13	16,67

ASIA	TOTAL	% (s/78)
China	2	2,56
the Philippines	1	1,28
India	5	6,41
Japan	1	1,28
the Middle East	2	2,56
Arab Countries	3	3,85
Syria	2	2,56
Thailand	3	3,85
Vietnam	1	1,28
ASIA TOTAL	20	25,64

EUROPE		
Germany	1	1,28
Austria	1	1,28
Spain	8	10,26
France	3	3,85
Greece	2	2,56
England	1	1,28
Italy	4	5,13
Norway	1	1,28
Netherlands	1	1,28
Portugal	3	3,85
Switzerland	1	1,28
Turkey	2	2,56
EUROPE TOTAL	28	35,90

TOTAL RESPONSES	78	100

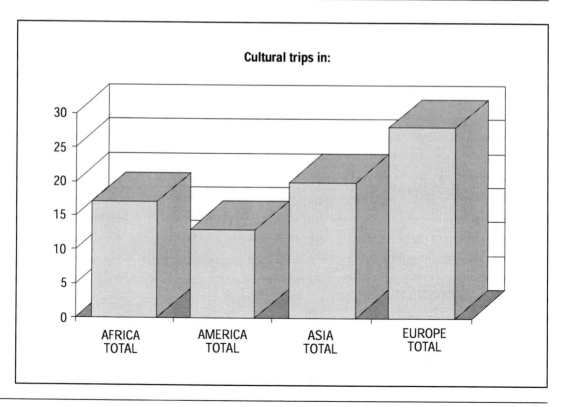

4.9.Stays with indigenous communities in:

ÁFRICA	TOTAL	% (s/27)
Burkina Faso	1	3,70
Mali	1	3,70
Morocco	4	14,81
Senegal	1	3,70
AFRICA TOTAL	7	25,93

AMERICA		
Argentina	1	3,70
Brazil (the Amazon)	3	11,11
Central America	3	11,11
Colombia	2	7,41
Mexico	1	3,70
Peru (Machu Pichu)	2	7,41
Santo Domingo	1	3,70
Venezuela	2	7,41
AMERICA TOTAL	15	55,56

ASIA		
India	1	3,70
Thailand	2	7,41
ASIA TOTAL	3	11,11

EUROPE		
Ireland (rural)	1	3,70
Turkey	1	3,70
EUROPE TOTAL	2	7,41

TOTAL RESPONSES	27	100

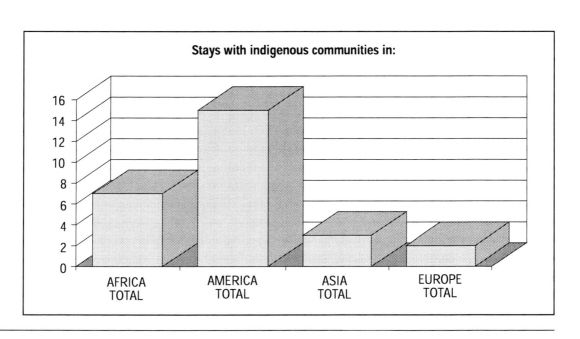

4.10. Handicrafts in:

AMERICA	TOTAL	% (s/16)
Brazil	1	6.25
Central America	3	18.75
Cuba	1	6.25
Mexico	2	12.5
AMERICA TOTAL	7	43.75

ASIA		
Thailand	2	12.5
ASIA TOTAL	2	12.5

EUROPE		
Spain	3	18.75
Greece	1	6.25
Portugal	1	6.25
Turkey	2	12.5
EUROPE TOTAL	7	43.75

TOTAL RESPONSES	16	100

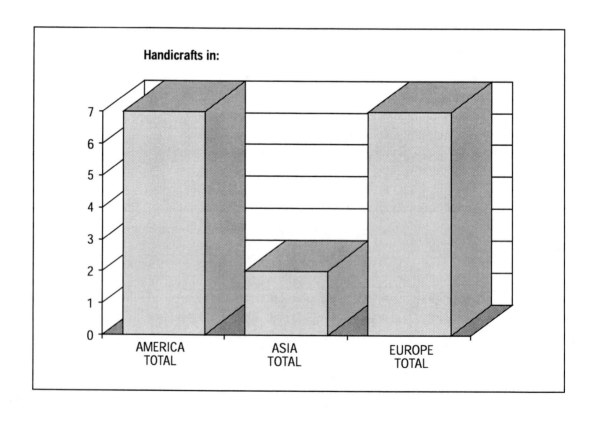

Handicrafts in:

4.11. Solidarity/Volunteer Tourism in:

	TOTAL		% (s/15)
AFRICA	1		6.67
AFRICA TOTAL		1	6.67
AMERICA			
Bolivia	1		6.67
Brazil	1		6.67
Ecuador	1		6.67
Guatemala	1		6.67
Mexico	1		6.67
Peru	2		13.33
AMERICA TOTAL		7	46.67
ASIA			
India	2		13.33
Nepal	1		6.67
ASIA TOTAL		3	20
EUROPE			
Spain	3		20
Turkey	1		6.67
EUROPE TOTAL		4	26.67
TOTAL RESPONSES		15	100

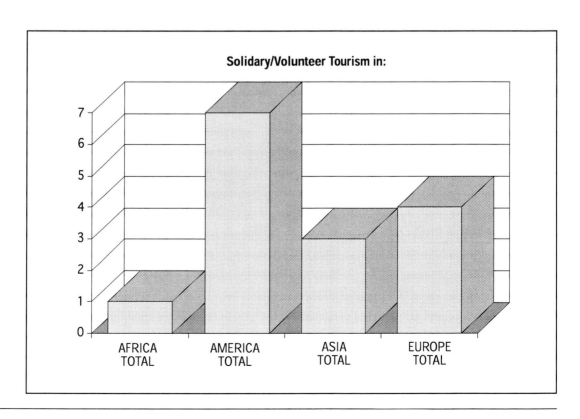

4.12. Sustainable hunting and fishing in:

AMERICA	TOTAL	% (s/7)
Brazil	1	14.29
Canada	1	14.29
Mexico	1	14.29
AMERICA TOTAL	3	42.86
EUROPE		
Spain	2	28.57
Greece	1	14.29
Turkey	1	14.29
EUROPE TOTAL	4	57.14
TOTAL RESPONSES	7	100

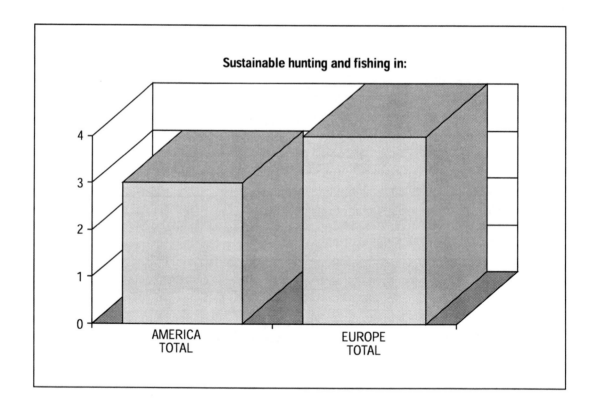

Sustainable hunting and fishing in:

4.13. Others:

Activities	TOTAL	% (s/18)
1. Archaeology/Paleontology	3	20
2. Rest/Relaxation	3	20
3. Studies	2	13.33
4. Cuisine	2	13.33
5. Monuments/Museums	2	13.33
6. Pleasure/Leisure	2	13.33
7. Safari	1	6.67
	15	100

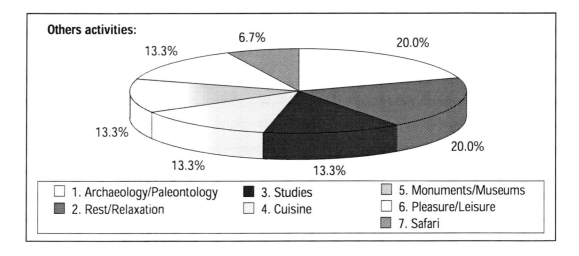

If not, why? (reasons):

	Total responses	% (s/68)
1. Lack of interest	9	13.24
2. Financial reasons	22	32.35
3. Lack of time or opportunity	17	25
4. Prefer other destinations (cultural tourism, sun and beach tourism, etc.	16	23.53
5. Others (no company, poor offer, small children, etc.)	4	5.88
	68	**100**

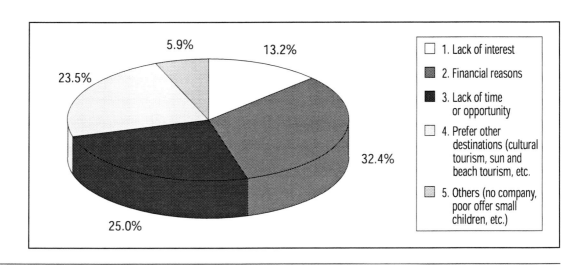

Annex 7:
Breakdown of question 5
of the tourist survey:

Which destinations interest you most for this type of trip? (Diagram16 in the report)

DISTANT AND EXOTIC DESTINATIONS:

AFRICA	TOTAL	% (s/484)
Africa in general	39	8.06
Algeria	1	0.21
Cape Verde	1	0.21
Egypt	19	3.93
Ethiopia	2	0.41
Kenya	7	1.45
Madagascar	1	0.21
Morocco	3	0.62
Namibia	1	0.21
South Africa	11	2.27
Tanzania	6	1.24
Tunisia	3	0.62
AFRICA TOTAL	94	19.42

DISTANT AND EXOTIC DESTINATIONS (Cont.):

AMERICA	TOTAL	% (s/484)
America in general	3	0.62
Alaska	2	0.41
Argentina	32	6.61
Belize	3	0.62
Bolivia	3	0.62
Brazil	32	6.61
Canada	9	1.86
Caribbean	15	3.10
Central America	11	2.27
Colombia	2	0.41
Costa Rica	12	2.48
Cuba	20	4.13
Chile	5	1.03
Ecuador	9	1.86
USA	10	2.07
Guatemala	4	0.83
the Galapagos Islands	2	0.41
Mexico	21	4.34
Paraguay	1	0.21
Peru	10	2.07
Dominican Republic	3	0.62
South America	33	6.82
Venezuela	8	1.65
AMERICA TOTAL	250	51.65

DISTANT AND EXOTIC DESTINATIONS (Cont.):

ASIA	TOTAL	% (s/484)
Asia in general	16	3.31
Bali	3	0.62
Bangladesh	1	0.21
Burma	1	0.21
China	10	2.07
Cyprus	2	0.41
the Philippines	1	0.21
the Persian Gulf	1	0.21
India	30	6.20
Indonesia	1	0.21
Iran	1	0.21
Israel	2	0.41
Japan	6	1.24
Jordan	4	0.83
Laos	1	0.21
the Maldives	3	0.62
Nepal	8	1.65
Near East	9	1.86
Polynesia	3	0.62
the Seychelles	5	1.03
Syria	1	0.21
the South of Asia	4	0.83
Thailand	11	2.27
Tibet	1	0.21
Vietnam	1	0.21
Yemen	1	0.21
ASIA TOTAL	111	22.93

OCEANIA	TOTAL	% (s/484)
Oceania in general	2	0.41
Australia	21	4.34
New Zealand	6	1.24
OCEANIA TOTAL	29	5.99

| DISTANT COUNTRIES TOTAL | 484 | 100 |

EUROPEAN DESTINATIONS:

	TOTAL	% (s/314)
Germany	10	3.18
The Alps	8	2.55
Austria	11	3.50
Belgium	3	0.96
Central Europe	8	2.55
Czech Republic	4	1.27
Denmark	2	0.64
Scandinavia	8	2.55
Finland	19	6.05
France	35	11.15
Great Britain	27	8.60
Greece	17	5.41
Holland	9	2.87
Hungary	2	0.64
Ireland	11	3.50
Iceland	11	3.50
Italy	46	14.65
Norway	36	11.46
Eastern European countries	9	2.87
Poland	1	0.32
Portugal	4	1.27
Russia	7	2.23
Sweden	4	1.27
Switzerland	9	2.87
Turkey	5	1.59
All	8	2.55
EUROPE TOTAL	**314**	**100**

SPANISH DESTINATIONS:

Comunities	TOTAL		% (s/133)
ANDALUSIA			
Cádiz	4		3.01
Córdoba	1		0.75
Granada	2		1.50
Seville	1		0.75
Andalusia in general	14		10.53
ANDALUSIA TOTAL		22	16.54
ARAGÓN			
The Aragón Pyrenees	1		0.75
Aragón in general	3		2.26
ARAGÓN TOTAL		4	3.01
ASTURIAS	21		15.79
ASTURIAS TOTAL	21		15.79
BALEARIC ISLANDS			
Ibiza	1		0.75
Majorca	1		0.75
Balearic Islands in general	2		1.50
BALEARIC ISLANDS TOTAL		4	3.01
CANARY ISLANDS			
El Hierro	1		0.75
La Gomera	1		0.75
La Palma	1		0.75
Lanzarote	1		0.75
Tenerife	4		3.01
Canary Islands in general	15		11.28
CANARY ISLANDS TOTAL		23	17.29
CANTABRIA	5		3.76
CANTABRIA TOTAL		5	3.76
CASTILLA-LEÓN			
Salamanca	3		2.26
Castilla-León in general	2		1.50
CASTILLA-LEÓN TOTAL		5	3.76

SPANISH DESTINATIONS (Cont):

Comunities	TOTAL		% (s/133)
CASTILLA LA MANCHA			
Albacete	1		0.75
Cuenca	1		0.75
Toledo	2		1.50
Castilla in general	4		3.01
CASTILLA-LA MANCHA TOTAL		9	6.77
CATALONIA			
Tarragona	1		0.75
Catalonia in general	7		5.26
CATALONIA TOTAL		8	6.02
EXTREMADURA	2		1.50
EXTREMADURA TOTAL		2	1.50
GALICIA			
Rías Bajas	1		0.75
Galicia gen.	12		9.02
Galicia in general		13	9.77
LA RIOJA	3		2.26
LA RIOJA TOTAL		3	2.26
MADRID			
Sierra	1		0.75
Madrid in general	3		2.26
MADRID TOTAL		4	3.01
MURCIA	2		1.50
MURCIA TOTAL		2	1.50
NAVARRE	2		1.50
NAVARRE TOTAL		2	1.50
BASQUE COUNTRY	2		1.50
BASQUE COUNTRY TOTAL		2	1.50
COMUNIDAD VALENCIANA			
Alicante	2		1.50
Comunidad Valenciana in general	3		2.26
COMUNIDAD VALENCIANA TOTAL		5	3.76
COMMUNITIES TOTAL	**133**		**100**

OTHER SPANISH DESTINATIONS:

	TOTAL	% (s/156)
Coasts	6	3.85
Islands	5	3.21
Mountains/Inland	10	6.41
The North of Spain	60	38.46
Doñana National Park	2	1.28
Picos de Europa National Park	5	3.21
Gredos Nature Reserve	5	3.21
Sierra de Cazorla Nature Reserve	3	1.92
The Pyrenees	13	8.33
The South of Spain	8	5.13
All Spain	36	23.08
Rural areas	3	1.92
TOTAL RESPONSES	**156**	**100**

Annex 8:
Québec Declaration on Ecotourism

In the framework of the UN International Year of Ecotourism, 2002, under the aegis of the United Nations Environment Programme (UNEP) and the World Tourism Organization (WTO), over one thousand participants coming from 132 countries, from the public, private and non-governmental sectors met at the World Ecotourism Summit, hosted in Québec City, Canada, by Tourisme Québec and the Canadian Tourism Commission, between 19 and 22 May 2002.

The Québec Summit represented the culmination of 18 preparatory meetings held in 2001 and 2002, involving over 3,000 representatives from national and local governments including the tourism, environment and other administrations, private ecotourism businesses and their trade associations, non-governmental organizations, academic institutions and consultants, intergovernmental organizations, and indigenous and local communities.

This document takes into account the preparatory process, as well as the discussions held during the Summit. It is the result of a multistakeholder dialogue, although it is not a negotiated document. Its main purpose is the setting of a preliminary agenda and a set of recommendations for the development of ecotourism activities in the context of sustainable development.

The participants at the Summit acknowledge the World Summit on Sustainable Development (WSSD) in Johannesburg, August/September 2002, as the ground-setting event for international policy in the next 10 years, and emphasize that, as a leading industry, the sustainability of tourism should be a priority at WSSD due to its potential contribution to poverty alleviation and environmental protection in endangered ecosystems. Participants therefore request the UN, its organizations and member governments represented at this Summit to disseminate the following Declaration and other results from the World Ecotourism Summit at the WSSD.

The participants to the World Ecotourism Summit, aware of the limitations of this consultative process to incorporate the input of the large variety of ecotourism stakeholders, particularly non-governmental organizations (NGOs) and local and indigenous communities,

Recognize that ecotourism embraces the principles of sustainable tourism, concerning the economic, social and environmental impacts of tourism. It also embraces the following specific principles which distinguish it from the wider concept of sustainable tourism:

- Contributes actively to the conservation of natural and cultural heritage,

- Includes local and indigenous communities in its planning, development and operation, and contributing to their well-being,

- Interprets the natural and cultural heritage of the destination to visitors,

- Lends itself better to independent travellers, as well as to organized tours for small size groups.

Acknowledge that tourism has significant and complex social, economic and environmental implications, which can bring both benefits and costs to the environment and local communities,

Consider the growing interest of people in travelling to natural areas, both on land and sea,

Recognize that ecotourism has provided a leadership role in introducing sustainability practices to the tourism sector,

Emphasize that ecotourism should continue to contribute to make the overall tourism industry more sustainable, by increasing economic and social benefits for host communities, actively contributing to the conservation of natural resources and the cultural integrity of host communities, and by increasing awareness of all travellers towards the conservation of natural and cultural heritage,

Recognize the cultural diversity associated with many natural areas, particularly because of the historical presence of local and indigenous communities, of which some have maintained their traditional knowledge, uses and practices many of which have proven to be sustainable over the centuries,

Reiterate that funding for the conservation and management of biodiverse and culturally rich protected areas has been documented to be inadequate worldwide,

Recognize further that many of these areas are home to peoples often living in poverty, who frequently lack adequate health care, education facilities, communications systems, and other infrastructure required for genuine development opportunity,

Affirm that different forms of tourism, especially ecotourism, if managed in a sustainable manner can represent a valuable economic opportunity for local and indigenous populations and their cultures and for the conservation and sustainable use of nature for future generations and can be a leading source of revenues for protected areas,

Emphasize that at the same time, wherever and whenever tourism in natural and rural areas is not properly planned, developed and managed, it contributes to the deterioration of natural landscapes, threats to wildlife and biodiversity, marine and coastal pollution, poor water quality, poverty, displacement of indigenous and local communities, and the erosion of cultural traditions,

Acknowledge that ecotourism development must consider and respect the land and property rights, and, where recognized, the right to self-determination and cultural sovereignty of indigenous and local communities, including their protected, sensitive and sacred sites as well as their traditional knowledge,

Stress that to achieve equitable social, economic and environmental benefits from ecotourism and other forms of tourism in natural areas, and to minimize or avoid potential negative impacts, participative planning mechanisms are needed that allow local and indigenous communities, in a transparent way, to define and regulate the use of their areas at the local level, including the right to opt out of tourism development,

Understand that small and micro businesses seeking to meet social and environmental objectives are key partners in ecotourism and are often operating in a development climate that does not provide suitable financial and marketing support for ecotourism,

Recognize that to improve the chances of survival of small-, medium-, and micro enterprises further understanding of the ecotourism market will be required through market research, specialized credit instruments for tourism businesses, grants for external costs, incentives for the use of sustainable energy and innovative technical solutions, and an emphasis on developing skills not only in business but within government and those seeking to support business solutions,

Accept the need to avoid discrimination between people, whether by race, gender or other personal circumstances, with respect to their involvement in ecotourism as consumers or suppliers,

Recognize that visitors have a responsibility to the sustainability of the destination and the global environment through their travel choice, behaviour and activities, and that therefore it is important to communicate to them the qualities and sensitivities of destinations,

In light of the above, the participants to the World Ecotourism Summit, having met in Québec City, from 19 to 22 May 2002, produced a series of recommendations, which they propose to governments, the private sector, non-governmental organizations, community-based associations, academic and research institutions, inter-governmental organizations, international financial institutions, development assistance agencies, and indigenous and local communities, as follows:

A. To national, regional and local governments

1. *formulate* national, regional and local ecotourism policies and development strategies that are consistent with the overall objectives of sustainable development, and to do so through a wide consultation process with those who are likely to become involved in, affect, or be affected by ecotourism activities;

2. *guarantee* -in conjunction with local and indigenous communities, the private sector, NGOs and all ecotourism stakeholders- the protection of nature, local and indigenous cultures and specially traditional knowledge, genetic resources, rights to land and property, as well as rights to water;

3. *ensure* the involvement, appropriate participation and necessary coordination of all the relevant public institutions at the national, provincial and local level, (including the establishment of inter-ministerial working groups as appropriate) at different stages in the ecotourism process, while at the same time opening and facilitating the participation of other stakeholders in ecotourism-related decisions. Furthermore, adequate budgetary mechanisms and appropriate legislative frameworks need to be set up to allow implementation of the objectives and goals set up by these multistakeholder bodies;

4. *include* in the above framework the necessary regulatory and monitoring mechanisms at the national, regional and local levels, including objective sustainability indicators jointly agreed with all stakeholders and environmental impact assessment studies to be used as feedback mechanism. Results of monitoring should be made available to the general public;

5. *develop* regulatory mechanisms for internalization of environmental costs in all aspects of the tourism product, including international transport;

6. *develop* the local and municipal capacity to implement growth management tools such as zoning, and participatory land-use planning not only in protected areas but in buffer zones and other ecotourism development zones;

7. *use* internationally approved and reviewed guidelines to develop certification schemes, ecolabels and other voluntary initiatives geared towards sustainability in ecotourism, encouraging private operators to join such schemes and promoting their recognition by consumers. However, certification systems should reflect regional and local criteria. Build capacity and provide financial support to make these schemes accessible to small and medium enterprises (SMEs). In addition, monitoring and a regulatory framework are necessary to support effective implementation of these schemes;

8. *ensure* the provision of technical, financial and human resources development support to micro, small and medium-sized firms, which are the core of ecotourism, with a view to enable them to start, grow and develop their businesses in a sustainable manner;

9. *define* appropriate policies, management plans, and interpretation programmes for visitors, and earmark adequate sources of funding for natural areas to manage visitor numbers, protect vulnerable ecosystems, and the sustainable use of sensitive habitats. Such plans should include clear norms, direct and indirect management strategies, and regulations with the funds to ensure monitoring of social and environmental impacts for all ecotourism businesses operating in the area, as well as for tourists wishing to visit them;

10. *include* micro, small and medium-sized ecotourism companies, as well as community-based and NGO-based ecotourism operations in the overall promotional strategies and programmes carried out by the National Tourism Administration, both in the international and domestic markets;

11. *encourage* and *support* the creation of regional networks and cooperation for promotion and marketing of ecotourism products at the international and national levels;

12. *provide* incentives to tourism operators and other service providers (such as marketing and promotion advantages) for them to adopt ecotourism principles and make their operations more environmentally, socially and culturally responsible;

13. *ensure* that basic environmental and health standards are identified and met by all ecotourism development even in the most rural areas. This should include aspects such as site selection, planning, design, the treatment of solid waste, sewage, and the protection of watersheds, etc., and ensure also that ecotourism development strategies are not undertaken by governments without investment in sustainable infrastructure and the reinforcement of local/municipal capabilities to regulate and monitor such aspects;

14. *institute* baseline environmental impact assessment (EIA) studies and surveys that record the social environmental state of destinations, with special attention to endangered species, and invest, or support institutions that invest in research programmes on ecotourism and sustainable tourism;

15. *support* the further implementation of the international principles, guidelines and codes of ethics for sustainable tourism (e.g. such as those proposed by UNEP, WTO, the Convention on Biological Diversity, the UN Commission on Sustainable Development and the International Labor Organization) for the enhancement of international and national legal frameworks, policies and master plans to implement the concept of sustainable development into tourism;

16. *consider* as one option the reallocation of tenure and management of public lands, from extractive or intensive productive sectors to tourism combined with conservation, wherever this is likely to improve the net social, economic and environmental benefit for the community concerned;

17. *promote* and *develop* educational programmes addressed to children and young people to enhance awareness about nature conservation and sustainable use, local and indigenous cultures and their relationship with ecotourism;

18. *promote* collaboration between outbound tour operators and incoming operators and other service providers and NGOs at the destination to further educate tourists and influence their behaviour at destinations, especially those in developing countries;

19. *incorporate* sustainable transportation principles in the planning and design of access and transportation systems, and encourage tour operators and the travelling public to make soft mobility choices.

B. To the private sector

20. bear in mind that for ecotourism businesses to be sustainable, they need to be profitable for all stakeholders involved, including the projects' owners, investors, managers and employees, as well as the communities and the conservation organizations of natural areas where it takes place;

21. *conceive, develop and conduct* their businesses minimizing negative effects on, and positively contributing to, the conservation of sensitive ecosystems and the environment in general, and directly benefiting and including local and indigenous communities;

22. *ensure* that the design, planning, development and operation of ecotourism facilities incorporates sustainability principles, such as sensitive site design and community sense of place, as well as conservation of water, energy and materials, and accessibility to all categories of population without discrimination;

23. *adopt* as appropriate a reliable certification or other systems of voluntary regulation, such as ecolabels, in order to demonstrate to their potential clients their adherence to sustainability principles and the soundness of the products and services they offer;

24. *cooperate* with governmental and non-governmental organizations in charge of protected natural areas and conservation of biodiversity, ensuring that ecotourism operations are practised according to the management plans and other regulations prevailing in those areas, so as to minimize any negative impacts upon them while enhancing the quality of the tourism experience and contribute financially to the conservation of natural resources;

25. *make* increasing use of local materials and products, as well as local logistical and human resource inputs in their operations, in order to maintain the overall authenticity of the ecotourism product and increase the proportion of financial and other benefits that remain at the destination. To achieve this, private operators should invest in the training of the local workforce;

26. *ensure* that the supply chain used in building up an ecotourism operation is thoroughly sustainable and consistent with the level of sustainability aimed at in the final product or service to be offered to the customer;

27. *work* actively with indigenous leadership and local communities to ensure that indigenous cultures and communities are depicted accurately and with respect, and that their staff and guests are well and accurately informed regarding local and indigenous sites, customs and history;

28. *promote* among their clients an ethical and environmentally conscious behaviour vis-à-vis the ecotourism destinations visited, such as by environmental education or by encouraging voluntary contributions to support local community or conservation initiatives;

29. *generate* awareness among all management and staff of local, national and global environmental and cultural issues through ongoing environmental education, and support the contribution that they and their families can make to conservation, community economic development and poverty alleviation;

30. *diversify* their offer by developing a wide range of tourist activities at a given destination and by extending their operations to different destinations in order to spread the potential benefits of ecotourism and to avoid overcrowding some selected ecotourism sites, thus threatening their long-term sustainability. In this regard, private operators are urged to respect, and contribute to, established visitor impact management systems of ecotourism destinations;

31. *create* and *develop* funding mechanisms for the operation of business associations or cooperatives that can assist with ecotourism training, marketing, product development, research and financing;

32. *ensure* an equitable distribution of financial benefits from ecotourism revenues between international, outbound and incoming tour operators, local service providers and local communities through appropriate instruments and strategic alliances;

33. *formulate* and *implement* company policies for sustainability with a view to applying them in each part of their operations.

C. To non-governmental organizations, community-based associations, academic and research institutions

34. *provide* technical, financial, educational, capacity building and other support to ecotourism destinations, host community organizations, small businesses and the corresponding local authorities in order to ensure that appropriate policies, development and management guidelines, and monitoring mechanisms are being applied towards sustainability;

35. *monitor* and *conduct* research on the actual impacts of ecotourism activities upon ecosystems, biodiversity, local and indigenous cultures and the socio-economic fabric of the ecotourism destinations;

36. *cooperate* with public and private organizations ensuring that the data and information generated through research is channeled to support decision-making processes in ecotourism development and management;

37. *cooperate* with research institutions to develop the most adequate and practical solutions to ecotourism development issues.

D. To inter-governmental organizations, international financial institutions and development assistance agencies

38. *develop* and *assist* in the implementation of national and local policy and planning guidelines and evaluation frameworks for ecotourism and its relationships with biodiversity conservation, socio-economic development, respect of human rights, poverty alleviation, nature conservation and other objectives of sustainable development, and to intensify the transfer of such know-how to all countries. Special attention should be paid to countries in a developing stage or least developed status, to small island developing States and to countries with mountain areas, considering that 2002 is also designated as the International Year of Mountains by the UN;

39. *build capacity* for regional, national and local organizations for the formulation and application of ecotourism policies and plans, based on international guidelines;

40. *develop or adopt, as appropriate,* international standards and financial mechanisms for ecotourism certification systems that take into account the needs of small and medium enterprises and facilitates their access to those procedures, and support their implementation;

41. *incorporate* multistakeholder dialogue processes into policies, guidelines and projects at the global, regional and national levels for the exchange of experiences between countries and sectors involved in ecotourism;

42. *strengthen* efforts in identifying the factors that determine the success or failure of ecotourism ventures throughout the world, in order to transfer such experiences and best practices to other nations, by means of publications, field missions, training seminars and technical assistance projects; UNEP, WTO and other international organizations should continue and expand the international dialogue after the Summit on sustainable tourism and ecotourism issues, for example by conducting periodical reviews of ecotourism development through international and regional forums;

43. *adapt* as necessary their financial facilities and lending conditions and procedures to suit the needs of micro-, small- and medium-sized ecotourism firms that are the core of this industry, as a condition to ensure its long term economic sustainability;

44. *develop* the internal human resource capacity to support sustainable tourism and ecotourism as a development sub-sector in itself and to ensure that internal expertise, research, and documentation are in place to oversee the use of ecotourism as a sustainable development tool;

45. *develop* financial mechanisms for training and capacity building, that takes into account the time and resources required to successfully enable local communities and indigenous peoples to participate equitably in ecotourism development.

E. To local and indigenous communities

In addition to all the references to local and indigenous communities made in the preceding paragraphs of this Declaration, (in particular para. 5, 8, 9 and 10 on page 2; para. 1 on page 3; in A 2 and 17; B 21 and 27; C 35; D 45) participants addressed the following recommendations to the local and indigenous communities themselves:

46. As part of a community vision for development, that may include ecotourism, *define* and *implement* a strategy for improving collective benefits for the community through ecotourism development including human, physical, financial, and social capital development, and improved access to technical information;

47. *strengthen, nurture* and *encourage* the community's ability to maintain and use traditional skills, particularly home-based arts and crafts, agricultural produce, traditional housing and landscaping that use local natural resources in a sustainable manner.

F. To the World Summit on Sustainable Development (WSSD)

48. *recognize* the need to apply the principles of sustainable development to tourism, and the exemplary role of ecotourism in generating economic, social and environmental benefits;

49. *integrate* the role of tourism, including ecotourism, in the outcomes expected at WSSD.

Québec City, Canada, 22 May 2002